WILLIAMS-SONOMA

Holiday
Celebrations

GENERAL EDITOR
Chuck Williams

RECIPES
Marie Simmons

PHOTOGRAPHY
Richard Eskite

TIME
LIFE
BOOKS

TIME-LIFE BOOKS

Time-Life Books is a division of Time Life Inc.
Time-Life is a trademark of Time Warner Inc. U.S.A

TIME-LIFE CUSTOM PUBLISHING
Vice President and Publisher: Terry Newell
Managing Editor: Donia Ann Steele
Director of Acquisitions: Jennifer L. Pearce
Vice President of Sales and Marketing: Neil Levin
Director of Financial Operations: J. Brian Birky

WILLIAMS-SONOMA
Founder and Vice Chairman: Chuck Williams
Book Buyer: Victoria Kalish

WELDON OWEN INC.
President: John Owen
Vice President and Publisher: Wendely Harvey
Chief Operating Officer: Larry Partington
Vice President International Sales: Stuart Laurence
Associate Publisher: Lisa Atwood
Senior Editor: Hannah Rahill
Consulting Editor: Norman Kolpas
Copy Editor: Sharon Silva
Design: Kari Perin, Perin+Perin
Production Director: Stephanie Sherman
Production Manager: Jen Dalton
Production Editor: Sarah Lemas
Editorial/Production Assistant: Cecily Upton
Food Stylist: George Dolese
Prop Stylist: Sara Slavin
Photo Production Coordinator: Juliann Harvey
Photo Assistant: Kevin Hossler
Food Styling Assistant: Jill Sorenson
Glossary Illustrations: Alice Harth

A NOTE ON WEIGHTS AND MEASURES
All recipes include customary U.S. and metric
measurements. Metric conversions are based on a
standard developed for these books and have been
rounded off. Actual weights may vary.

The Williams-Sonoma Lifestyles series
conceived and produced by Weldon Owen Inc.
814 Montgomery Street, San Francisco, CA 94133

In collaboration with Williams-Sonoma
3250 Van Ness Avenue, San Francisco, CA 94109

Separations by Colourscan Overseas Co. Pte. Ltd.
Printed in Singapore by Tien Wah Press (Pte.) Ltd.

A WELDON OWEN PRODUCTION
Copyright © 1998 Weldon Owen Inc.
All rights reserved, including the right of reproduc-
tion in whole or in part in any form.

First printed in 1998
10 9 8 7 6 5 4 3 2 1

Library of Congress
Cataloging-in-Publication Data

Simmons, Marie.
    Holiday celebrations / general editor, Chuck
Williams; recipes, Marie Simmons; photography
by Richard Eskite.
        p. cm. — (Williams-Sonoma lifestyles)
    Includes index.
    ISBN 0-7835-4618-1
    1. Holiday Cookery   I. Williams, Chuck.
    II. Simmons, Marie.   III. Series.
TX739.H628   1998
641.5'68— dc21   98-9546
                                  CIP

A NOTE ON NUTRITIONAL ANALYSIS
Each recipe is analyzed for significant nutrients per
serving. Not included in the analysis are ingredients
that are optional or added to taste, or are suggested
as an alternative or substitution either in the recipe
or in the recipe introduction or accompanying tip. In
recipes that yield a range of servings, the analysis is
for the middle of that range.

Contents

Welcome

At no other time of year are we more likely to entertain on a grand scale than during the holidays. It is, after all, the season of celebration, whether we're gathering around the Thanksgiving table, decking the halls at Christmas, lighting the Hanukkah candles, or ringing in the New Year.

Making holidays memorable does not necessarily mean extravagant preparations, however. Looking back over festive seasons past, the ones I recall most vividly are those at which the hosts were able to enjoy the party as much as the guests. It didn't matter whether the food served was a feast that had taken all day to cook or a quickly prepared light repast. What meant the most was an air of ease, merriment, and warmth enjoyed by all.

Helping you to create just such an ambience is the aim of this book. On the following pages, you'll find a wealth of ideas on how to set a festive scene. The remainder of the book consists of 50 recipes from which you can compose countless holiday menus.

Feel free to use any of the ideas or recipes in this book in whichever way best suits your own personal style. And whatever your occasion for celebration might be, I wish you happy holidays!

Chuck Williams

Setting the Holiday Scene

Seasonal decorations can take delightfully varied forms. Individual candles can be arranged into the traditional Hanukkah menorah configuration (top). Your own garden, nurseries, or produce shops can yield an array of boughs and seasonal fruits and vegetables (top, right). Forcing vases transform holiday bulbs (above), such as paperwhite narcissus and amaryllis, into bright harbingers of spring. And sprigs of greenery can turn a year-round chandelier (opposite) into a spectacular holiday display.

Transforming Your Home

Holidays, more than any other time of year, lead people not merely to decorate their homes but to transform them. Creating a holiday-inspired environment helps to capture the magic of the season, whether your aim is to underscore the heartwarming welcome of Thanksgiving, the joy of Christmas, the illumination of Hanukkah, or the bright hopes of the New Year.

The best way to make that transformation complete is to involve all the senses with decorations, candlelight, pleasing aromas, and festive music. That doesn't mean that your efforts must be done on any sort of grand scale, however. Even a few simple touches can express the spirit of the season.

Creating Beautiful Sights

Seasonal-inspired displays of greenery, flowers, vegetables and fruits, ornaments, and curios are the most popular way to transform a home's interior for the holidays. A fireplace mantel or hearth offers the most time-honored setting for such arrangements, but so, too, do a wide variety of other eye-catching sites, from doorways to windowsills, side tables to chandeliers.

Traditional greenery brings in the heady scent of the outdoors with boughs, garlands, swags, and wreaths of aromatic white pine, fir, blue spruce, cedar, and eucalyptus. Olive branches, boxwood, and bay leaves also offer long-lasting texture and fragrance. Add your own embellishments inspired by the specific holiday: colorful autumn leaves, winter squashes, and gourds for Thanksgiving; blue and white candles for Hanukkah; or favorite Christmas ornaments or tableaux. Include ribbons in suitable holiday colors. And don't forget the beauty flowers can add. Look beyond traditional poinsettias for cut flowers like cyclamen, gardenia, and tea roses, and seasonal bulbs such as amaryllis, paperwhite narcissus, hyacinth, crocus, daffodils, and tulips.

Candles will literally cast your home in a whole new light. Today, stores and catalogs offer them in an incredible range of colors, shapes, and sizes. Among the options to seek out are candles embedded with seasonal greenery and flowers; small candles that you can float in a decorative bowl of water along with fresh cranberries; slender textured beeswax tapers for an elegant New Year's Eve; pretty oil lamps resembling glass Christmas balls; and innovative contemporary variations on Hanukkah menorahs (see photo at left). The warm glow of luminarias, small votives set in sand inside paper bags, can illuminate a deck, garden, or outdoor staircase.

Providing Sounds of the Season

To help establish a festive mood, stop at a good music store on one of your shopping rounds. Look for seasonal recordings that offer a variety of styles—jazz, blues, classical, choral, rock and roll—on a single CD, or select less eclectic recordings to match your tastes and the tastes of your guests, such as arias for a group of opera enthusiasts.

Also, consider an old-fashioned alternative: the sing-along. If you have a piano and you or a guest knows how to play, sheet music or songbooks provide a wealth of popular tunes. Be sure to photocopy the lyric sheets so everyone can join in.

SEASONAL SCENTS

The aromas emanating from your stove while you cook the holiday meal will go a long way toward creating a festive spirit in your kitchen and dining room. With little extra effort, however, you can also heighten the seasonal scent in other rooms.

One of the easiest ways to scent a room is with aromatic potpourri. Create your own by tossing together cedar chips, cinnamon sticks, dried citrus peel, cloves, and the like and placing the mixture in bowls. Florist and specialty shops sell such mixtures ready-made.

Or scent the space with an aromatic brew, made or just kept hot on a portable burner in the room. Add a few cinnamon sticks, whole cloves and allspice berries, and strips of orange peel to plain water or—if you'd like to drink the concoction—to sweet or hard cider. Simmer briefly to activate the aromas.

Decorating the Holiday Table

Festivity reigns supreme on a table set for the New Year, complete with paper hats, noisemakers, and other party favors. Of course, a bottle of vintage champagne is on ice, ready to pop open and pour at the stroke of midnight.

Making Practical Preparations

Holiday meals call for us to pay a little more attention than we ordinarily do to decorating and setting the dining table.

The logical place to begin is with the table itself. If you have a formal dining room or a beautiful dining table, this is the time to use it. Consider polishing it up if the top is especially attractive, or pull out a festive tablecloth. If you plan to have more guests than the table can seat, move in tables from other rooms. Or consider staging your party as a buffet (see page 13) instead of a more elaborate sit-down meal.

Creating the Centerpiece

Outmoded tradition too often dictates that holiday centerpieces are imposing, expensive, and hard-to-assemble compositions of flowers, foliage, and other decorations that crowd the table and block the views of the guests. Logic and imagination, however, can free you from such constructions forever.

Try thinking of your holiday centerpiece as a landscape that runs the length of the table, full of pleasing and varied features for every guest to enjoy. If you wish, begin by placing a runner—a wide strip of opulent cloth, fabric, or ribbon—lengthwise along the center of the table, to act as a backdrop. Then add other embellishments to your liking. A bowl of ornaments (see photo at right), for example, captures the festive spirit of Christmas, as would other holiday-themed objects, such as small Thanksgiving-inspired turkey figurines, an assortment

Each in its own way, three different centerpieces capture the spirit of the season: an assortment of sugared fruits (far left), arrayed like jewels in a pedestal bowl; a landscape of wintry produce punctuated by citrus-colored pillar candles (center); and votive candles flickering amid flats of freshly sprouted wheat grass (left), hinting at the season of rebirth to come.

of the four-sided Hanukkah tops known as *dreidls,* or a jumble of New Year's party hats, streamers, and noisemakers. Some of your favorite collectibles could contribute their own uniquely personal touch. Selections from the season's harvest, particularly small winter squashes and gourds, tawny pears, persimmons, dried ears of corn, and bundled wheat sheaves, are among the loveliest holiday table appointments.

Flowers and candles, of course, are the most common decorative elements. Red tulips, miniature white, mango, and burgundy calla lilies, chocolate cosmos, and chartreuse lady's mantle are commonly available in winter months and can make a striking arrangement, either in elegant bouquets of a single variety or in dramatic combinations of vivid color. Take care not to include heavily scented blossoms or

candles that might interfere with your guests' appreciation of the food and wine you serve.

Whatever items you decide upon, include objects of different heights to give the landscape greater interest. Do not, however, get carried away with your decorations, despite the countless options available. Simplicity usually expresses seasonal sentiments with the greatest eloquence.

If you plan to serve the meal family style, allow room for your serving platters and bowls; you might even want to place them on the table beforehand in a dry run, so you can arrange the decorations around them. Plan on space for the bottles of wine you'll be pouring, including an ice bucket for white wine and champagne.

Setting the Place

Many opportunities present themselves for making guests feel welcome at the holiday table. Small gifts with name tags (above) or individual bud vases (below) may designate each person's place. The finest family silver, china, and crystal (center) compose a formal setting for an elegant meal, while a more casual setting (right) gains a touch of flair with a purple martini glass and a miniature frame.

Making Guests Feel Welcome

Whenever we entertain, we want to make our guests feel welcome. The holiday season offers us an opportunity to do just that as we prepare individual place settings at the dinner table.

Of course, you should let the menu itself (see pages 16–17 for suggestions) tell you what you'll need at each place in the way of dishes, cutlery, and glassware. If you have a special set of holiday dishes, by all means use it. Press into service your best china, silver, crystal, linens, and any heirloom pieces; or use other items, from Italian pottery to bistro ware, that reflect your own personal entertaining style. Individual salt cellars and pepper shakers can be an elegant enhancement.

When it comes to setting individual places, think of each as a personal welcome to the guest who will be sitting there. Feel free to assign seats in advance, giving thought to which arrangements might spark enjoyable conversation for everyone at the table. Simple cards, whether standing on their own or attached to small gifts, can mark each place. To get the party off to an even livelier start, furnish each place setting with a small ornament or favor that reflects an individual guest's interests—a ceramic cat for a cat lover, a ribbon-wrapped golf ball for a golf fanatic, a doll-sized rolling pin for an enthusiastic baker, and so on—and let everyone hunt for his or her special spot.

Arranging a Buffet

Entertaining with Ease
When you have a large crowd
to feed, or you simply wish to
celebrate the holidays in a more
casual fashion, a buffet is ideal.
With all the dishes prepared in
advance or carefully coordinated
to be ready around the same
time, your work is largely finished, and you are free—apart
from the customary attention
to last-minute details—to enjoy
more of the party yourself.

Planning a buffet begins with
the menu. Choose dishes that
guests can serve themselves
from platters or bowls and eat
with little fear of spillage: bite-
sized appetizers; soups that are
easily ladled into and eaten from
mugs; salads and accompaniments that can be scooped up
with a single large spoon; main
dishes that are carved in advance; and desserts in individual
portions. As you would when
planning any menu, give some
thought to offering a pleasing
variety of colors, flavors, textures, and temperatures.

For presenting these dishes,
you'll need large bowls, platters,
trays, tureens, and appropriate

serving tools. Plan ahead for
ways to keep hot dishes hot,
using warming trays, chafing
dishes, and oven-to-tableware—
and have trivets on hand to
protect your table. Plan well in
advance, so you'll have time to
buy, borrow, or rent pieces you
might be lacking.

Your dinner table itself can
be used for the buffet. Alternatively, you can press into
service any other large surface,
including sideboards, coffee or
sofa tables, or kitchen counters.
Think ahead about how traffic
will flow as guests serve themselves, moving tables away
from walls or other furniture
to provide access from all sides.
For large parties, you might
want to divide the buffet among
several different stations, offering soup or appetizers and
beverages in one area, main
courses and sides in another,
and desserts and hot drinks in
a third. Wherever you stage the
buffet, include close at hand
everything your guests will
need: stacks of dishes, bundles
of napkins and cutlery, wine-
glasses, and so on.

Beauty and practicality join forces in
holiday buffet preparations. A "bouquet"
of napkins holds cutlery (top), while
colored ribbons help guests keep track
of their wine glasses. An assortment of
sturdy pedestals (above) gives a buffet
table both dramatic dimension and
enhanced accessibility.

Beverages

If you don't have the time for a full-scale holiday dinner, consider hosting an afternoon tea party. Offer baked goods along with a selection of different teas, each labeled with a decorative hand-lettered card that explains its characteristics.

Hot Double-Apple Cider

If the apple slices are very dry, you might need to add more cider after they have had a chance to rehydrate.

6–8 cups (48–64 fl oz/1.5–2 l) apple cider
2 cups (16 fl oz/500 ml) water
½ cup (2 oz/60 g) packed moist dried apple slices
8 cinnamon sticks
⅛ teaspoon ground cloves

❋ In a large saucepan over medium heat, combine the apple cider, water, apple slices, cinnamon sticks, and cloves. Bring to a simmer, cover, remove from the heat, and let stand for 15 minutes to rehydrate the apples.

❋ Return the saucepan to medium heat. Reheat for 5 minutes. Ladle into mugs, distributing the apple slices and cinnamon sticks evenly.

SERVES 8

Hot Spiced Rum Lemonade

Warm the hearts and souls of your guests by serving mugs of this spicy hot lemonade, fragrant with cloves and heady with rum.

4 orange zest strips, each 3 inches (7.5 cm) long and ½ inch (12 mm) wide
4 whole cloves
4 cups (32 fl oz/1 l) water
½ cup (4 oz/125 g) sugar

juice of 4 large lemons, strained (about ½ cup/4 fl oz/125 ml)
½ cup (4 fl oz/125 ml) light rum

❋ Twist each zest strip gently to form a soft curl, then pierce with a whole clove. Set aside.

❋ In a saucepan, bring the water to a boil. Add the sugar and stir until dissolved. Remove from the heat. Stir in the lemon juice. Pour into mugs, dividing evenly. Add 2 tablespoons rum to each mug. Garnish each drink with a curl of orange zest and serve at once.

SERVES 4

Holiday Cosmopolitan

A few frozen cranberries added to each glass make this festive cocktail especially merry.

1½ cups (12 fl oz/375 ml) cranberry juice cocktail, chilled
¾ cup (6 fl oz/180 ml) lemon vodka or regular vodka, chilled
3 tablespoons bottled sweetened lime juice (Rose's brand)
3 tablespoons triple sec or Cointreau
8–10 ice cubes
¼ cup (1 oz/30 g) frozen cranberries

❋ In a large pitcher, combine the cranberry juice cocktail, vodka, lime juice, and triple sec or Cointreau. Add the ice cubes and stir to mix well. Strain into martini glasses. Garnish each serving with a few frozen cranberries.

SERVES 6

Classic Eggnog

Cooking the eggs makes this eggnog smooth and mellow.

4 cups (32 fl oz/1 l) milk
6 eggs
⅓ cup (3 oz/90 g) sugar
pinch of salt
1 teaspoon vanilla extract (essence)
1 cup (8 fl oz/250 ml) chilled heavy (double) cream
½ cup (4 fl oz/125 ml) brandy, or to taste (optional)
dash of ground cinnamon
dash of ground nutmeg

❋ In a small saucepan over medium heat, warm the milk just until it is very hot, about 5 minutes.

❋ In a large saucepan, combine the eggs, sugar, and salt. Whisk until well blended. Gradually stir in 2 cups (16 fl oz/500 ml) of the hot milk. Place over low heat and cook, stirring constantly, until the mixture is thick enough to coat a metal spoon with a thin film or until it registers 160°F (71°C) on an instant-read thermometer, about 10 minutes. Remove from the heat and stir in the remaining 2 cups (16 fl oz/500 ml) hot milk and the vanilla. Cover, placing plastic wrap directly on the surface, and refrigerate until thoroughly chilled, at least 3 hours or as long as overnight.

❋ Just before serving, pour the cream into a large bowl. Using an electric beater, beat until soft peaks form. Stir ½ cup (4 fl oz/125 ml) brandy, if using, into the chilled eggnog. Taste and add more as needed. Using a rubber spatula, gently fold the whipped cream into the eggnog just until no white streaks remain. Pour into a punch bowl, then sprinkle with the cinnamon and nutmeg.

SERVES 12

Apricot-Champagne Cocktail

Throughout the holiday season, welcome close friends with a sparkling glass of bubbly.

½ cup (4 fl oz/125 ml) apricot brandy, chilled
1 bottle (24 fl oz/750 ml) champagne or other sparkling white wine, chilled
8 fresh or frozen raspberries or 2 large strawberries, halved

❋ Divide the brandy evenly among 4 champagne flutes. Slowly add the champagne, filling each glass. Garnish each serving with 2 raspberries or a strawberry half. Serve at once.

SERVES 4

Planning Menus

The recipes in this book can be mixed and matched to create a wide variety of dinner menus for the holiday season. The 10 examples presented here express only a handful of the many combinations you can put together. When planning any holiday dinner, keep tradition in mind, while choosing courses whose ingredients, seasonings, textures, and colors complement one another. Add other components as you wish, such as appetizers, green salads, vegetable accompaniments, fresh-baked breads, and beverages.

Contemporary Thanksgiving

Cornmeal-Crusted Oysters
with Sour Cream and Caviar
PAGE 35

Glazed Turkey Breast with
Corn Bread Stuffing
PAGE 69

Caramelized Pear, Lemon,
and Currant Tart
PAGE 93

Homespun Christmas Eve

Sweet and White Potato Gratin
PAGE 77

Baked Ham with Orange-
Mustard-Pepper Glaze
PAGE 66

Country-Style Brandied Apple
and Dried Cherry Tart
PAGE 105

New Year's Day Dinner

Three-Mushroom Chowder
with Roasted Red Pepper Purée
PAGE 44

Curried Cornish Hens with
Spiced Confetti Couscous
PAGE 70

Chocolate Roulade with
Chocolate Brandy Sauce
PAGE 94

Holiday Buffet Supper

Gorgonzola and
Toasted Pecan Filo Rolls
PAGE 27

Apple-Stuffed Pork Loin
with Cider Sauce
PAGE 55

Ginger Sour Cream
Cheesecake
PAGE 98

Seafood Repast

Pan-Seared Scallops with
Apple-Onion Marmalade
PAGE 51

Maple-Glazed Salmon
Fillet with Oven-Roasted
Sweet Potatoes
PAGE 65

Cranberry-Raspberry Granita
PAGE 89

Vegetarian Winter Feast

Mushroom Crostini
PAGE 23

Winter White Lasagne
PAGE 60

Apricot and Cinnamon
Soufflés
PAGE 106

Hanukkah Party

Potato Pancakes with Smoked
Salmon and Sour Cream
PAGE 24

Beef Brisket with Caramelized
Onions and Merlot Sauce
PAGE 73

Caramelized Cashew Tartlets
with Maple Whipped Cream
PAGE 102

Elegant New Year's Eve

Seafood Bisque
PAGE 48

Venison Loin with
Mushroom Sauce
PAGE 59

Toasted Hazelnut
Chocolate Custard
PAGE 90

Traditional Thanksgiving

Acorn Squash and
Sweet Potato Soup with
Walnut-Parsley Pesto
PAGE 31

Roasted Turkey
with Barley Stuffing
PAGE 56

Pumpkin Praline Pie
PAGE 101

Fireside Christmas Dinner

Smoked Herring and Cream
Cheese Pâté with Dill
PAGE 19

Roast Duck with Cranberry
Glaze and Cranberry Relish
PAGE 62

Steamed Fig Pudding with
Orange-Caramel Cream Sauce
PAGE 97

Smoked Herring and Cream Cheese Pâté with Dill

PREP TIME: 20 MINUTES, PLUS
1 HOUR FOR CHILLING

INGREDIENTS

½ lb (250 g) smoked herring, patted dry, larger bones and skin removed, and fish broken up

1 lb (500 g) cream cheese, at room temperature

¼ cup (1 oz/30 g) chopped shallots

2 tablespoons lemon juice

2 tablespoons snipped fresh dill, plus sprigs for garnish (optional)

1 teaspoon grated lemon zest

2 or 3 heads Belgian endive (chicory/witloof)

salmon caviar (optional)

MAKE-AHEAD TIP: The pâté can be made up to 3 days in advance. Cover tightly and refrigerate until you are ready to fill the leaves.

Smoked herring, sometimes called kippers, are fresh herring that have been split, salted, dried, and then cold smoked. The smoky taste of the fish and the creaminess of the cheese make this a sophisticated appetizer for all your holiday entertaining.

MAKES 24 PIECES; SERVES 8–12

❊ In a food processor, combine the smoked herring, cream cheese, shallots, lemon juice, snipped dill, and lemon zest. Process until smooth. Scrape into a bowl, cover, and chill for about 1 hour.

❊ Meanwhile, trim the bases from the endives, and separate the leaves. You will need 24 leaves. Place in a bowl, add cold water just to cover, and drop in a few ice cubes. Chill.

❊ When the pâté is chilled, drain the leaves, pat them dry, and spoon 1 generous tablespoon of the pâté onto each leaf. Alternatively, spoon the chilled pâté into a pastry (piping) bag fitted with a large rosette tip, and pipe a rosette in the center of the leaf or pipe a strip along the length of the leaf. If desired, garnish each leaf with a dill sprig and a small spoonful of salmon caviar.

❊ Arrange the filled leaves on a platter and serve, or cover and refrigerate for up to 3 hours before serving. Serve chilled.

NUTRITIONAL ANALYSIS PER PIECE: Calories 84 (Kilojoules 353); Protein 3 g; Carbohydrates 1 g; Total Fat 8 g; Saturated Fat 4 g; Cholesterol 27 mg; Sodium 126 mg; Dietary Fiber 0 g

Gruyère Herb Puffs

PREP TIME: 25 MINUTES

COOKING TIME: 40 MINUTES

INGREDIENTS

¼ cup (2 oz/60 g) unsalted butter

½ cup (4 fl oz/125 ml) water

⅔ cup (3½ oz/105 g) all-purpose (plain) flour

½ teaspoon salt

3 eggs, at room temperature

1 cup (4 oz/125 g) shredded Gruyère cheese

1 tablespoon fresh thyme leaves

1 teaspoon minced fresh rosemary leaves

1 teaspoon hot-pepper sauce such as Tabasco

MAKE-AHEAD TIP: These puffs freeze well, making them ideal for holiday meals when advance preparation is invaluable. Bake as directed, let cool completely, and freeze in a single layer. Transfer to a lock-top bag and freeze for up to 4 weeks; thaw at room temperature for about 1 hour, then place on a baking sheet in a 350°F (180°C) oven to crisp for about 10 minutes.

These pretty little puffs are made from choux pastry, which is also used for cream puffs.

MAKES 24 PUFFS; SERVES 6–8

❋ Preheat an oven to 400°F (200°C). Butter a large baking sheet.

❋ In a saucepan over medium heat, combine the butter and water. Heat until the butter melts and the water boils, about 3 minutes. Add the flour and salt and stir vigorously with a wooden spoon until the mixture leaves the sides of the pan and forms a ball. Remove from the heat and let cool for 3 minutes.

❋ Using a wooden spoon or a handheld electric mixer on medium speed, beat in the eggs, one at a time, beating well after each addition. The batter should have a dull sheen. Stir in the cheese, thyme, rosemary, and hot-pepper sauce until well mixed.

❋ Drop the batter by rounded tablespoonfuls onto the prepared baking sheet, allowing about 2 inches (5 cm) between the mounds. Alternatively, spoon the batter into a pastry (piping) bag fitted with a large rosette tip and pipe mounds of batter onto the baking sheet.

❋ Bake for 15 minutes. Reduce the oven temperature to 350°F (180°C) and continue to bake until puffed and golden, about 15 minutes longer. Remove from the oven and let cool on the baking sheet set on a rack. Arrange in a basket or on a tray. Serve warm or at room temperature.

NUTRITIONAL ANALYSIS PER PUFF: Calories 62 (Kilojoules 260); Protein 3 g; Carbohydrates 3 g; Total Fat 4 g; Saturated Fat 2 g; Cholesterol 37 mg; Sodium 79 mg; Dietary Fiber 0 g

Mushroom Crostini

PREP TIME: 35 MINUTES

COOKING TIME: 40 MINUTES

INGREDIENTS

FOR THE CROSTINI

½ cup (4 fl oz/125 ml) olive oil

24 slices coarse country bread, each about ½ inch (12 mm) thick and 3 inches (7.5 cm) in diameter

1 clove garlic, halved

FOR THE MUSHROOM SPREAD

5 tablespoons (3 fl oz/80 ml) extra-virgin olive oil

½ lb (250 g) fresh white button mushrooms, brushed clean and chopped

¼ lb (125 g) fresh cremini mushrooms, brushed clean and chopped

¼ lb (125 g) fresh shiitake mushrooms, brushed clean, stems discarded, and chopped

2 cloves garlic, finely chopped

2 tablespoons finely chopped fresh flat-leaf (Italian) parsley, plus whole leaves for garnish (optional)

2 teaspoons fresh thyme leaves or ½ teaspoon dried thyme

½ teaspoon minced fresh rosemary or ¼ teaspoon dried rosemary

1 teaspoon coarse salt, plus salt to taste

ground pepper to taste

¼ cup (1¼ oz/37 g) drained, oil-packed sun-dried tomatoes, finely chopped, plus sun-dried tomato slivers for garnish (optional)

Use any combination of fresh mushrooms as long as the total weight is 1 pound (500 g). Both the crostini and mushroom spread can be made ahead, which makes this a perfect recipe for the busy holiday season.

MAKES 24 CROSTINI; SERVES 12

❋ Preheat an oven to 350°F (180°C). To make the crostini, lightly brush olive oil on both sides of each bread slice. Arrange the bread in a single layer on a baking sheet.

❋ Bake until the crostini are golden on the edges, about 25 minutes. Remove from the oven and let cool slightly. Using the cut side of the garlic, lightly rub one side over each slice of bread. Set aside. The crostini can be made up to 1 week ahead and stored in an airtight container.

❋ To make the mushroom spread, heat 2 tablespoons of the olive oil in a large frying pan over medium-high heat. Add all the mushrooms and cook, stirring often, until lightly browned, about 10 minutes. Add the garlic, chopped parsley, thyme, rosemary, 1 teaspoon salt, and pepper. Cook, stirring, for 2 minutes longer.

❋ Transfer the mushroom mixture to a food processor. Process until very finely chopped. With the processor running, add the remaining 3 tablespoons olive oil in a thin, steady stream, processing until the mixture is smooth and spreadable. Transfer to a bowl and stir in the chopped sun-dried tomatoes. Season with salt and pepper. The mushroom spread can be made up to 1 day ahead and stored, covered, in the refrigerator. Bring to room temperature before serving.

❋ Spread each piece of bread with about 1 tablespoon of the mushroom mixture. Arrange on a platter and, if desired, garnish each with a parsley leaf and/or a sliver of sun-dried tomato.

NUTRITIONAL ANALYSIS PER PIECE: Calories 152 (Kilojoules 638); Protein 3 g; Carbohydrates 16 g; Total Fat 9 g; Saturated Fat 1 g; Cholesterol 0 mg; Sodium 236 mg; Dietary Fiber 1 g

Yukon Gold Potato Pancakes with Chives, Smoked Salmon, and Sour Cream

PREP TIME: 30 MINUTES

COOKING TIME: 25 MINUTES

INGREDIENTS

1¾ lb (875 g) Yukon Gold or other yellow-fleshed potatoes, peeled

1 small yellow onion, grated

1 egg, lightly beaten

2 tablespoons matzo meal

1 teaspoon salt

ground pepper to taste

2 tablespoons snipped fresh chives, plus extra for garnish (optional)

½ cup (4 oz/125 g) solid vegetable shortening, or as needed

2 oz (60 g) sliced smoked salmon, cut into 1-inch (2.5-cm) squares

¼ cup (2 fl oz/60 ml) sour cream

salmon caviar (optional)

COOKING TIP: Veteran *latke* makers say the secret to perfect crisp potato pancakes is to squeeze as much moisture as possible from the grated potato, and to fry the pancakes in vegetable shortening rather than oil.

Crisp potato pancakes, or *latkes*, are classics of the Hanukkah table. Today, there are many variations on this pancake tradition. Some include shredded zucchini (courgettes), others sweet potatoes, and still others are seasoned with green (spring) onion and sesame seeds. Here is a fancy version made with Yukon Gold potatoes and topped with smoked salmon.

MAKES ABOUT 24 BITE-SIZED PANCAKES; SERVES 6–8

❈ Using the medium-fine holes of a handheld grater, grate the potatoes into a large bowl. Transfer to a sieve and, using the back of a spoon, press out the excess moisture. Then squeeze the potatoes with your hand to extract more moisture.

❈ Place the grated potatoes in a bowl and add the onion, egg, matzo meal, salt, and pepper. Stir to blend. Fold in the 2 tablespoons chives.

❈ In a heavy frying pan over medium-high heat, melt the ½ cup (4 oz/125 g) shortening until the surface ripples. Working in batches and being careful not to crowd the pan, measure out 1 level tablespoon batter for each pancake and drop it into the hot oil. Fry until crisp and golden on the first side, about 4 minutes. Turn and fry on the second side until golden, about 4 minutes longer. Transfer to paper towels to drain. Keep warm until all the batter has been used. Add more shortening to the pan if needed.

❈ When all the pancakes have been cooked, arrange on a warmed platter. Top each with a square of smoked salmon, and then top the salmon with ½ teaspoon sour cream. If desired, sprinkle each with a few pieces of the remaining snipped chives or a small spoonful of caviar. Serve warm.

NUTRITIONAL ANALYSIS PER PANCAKE: Calories 81 (Kilojoules 340); Protein 1 g; Carbohydrates 6 g; Total Fat 6 g; Saturated Fat 2 g; Cholesterol 10 mg; Sodium 122 mg; Dietary Fiber 1 g

Gorgonzola, Apple, and Toasted Pecan Filo Rolls

PREP TIME: 30 MINUTES

COOKING TIME: 35 MINUTES

INGREDIENTS

1 cup (4 oz/125 g) pecans, finely chopped

1 cup (4 oz/125 g) peeled, cored, and finely chopped Golden Delicious or other firm cooking apple

¼ lb (125 g) Gorgonzola cheese, crumbled

2 tablespoons all-purpose (plain) flour

12 sheets filo dough, thawed in the refrigerator if frozen

½ cup (4 oz/125 g) unsalted butter, melted and cooled

freshly ground pepper to taste

COOKING TIP: This same cheese mixture can be used as a filling for filo triangles or layered in a pan with filo sheets. Cut into squares before cooking, and then bake until golden.

The rich flavor of toasted nuts enhances this special holiday treat. Almost any cheese, crisp fruit, or nuts make a delicious filling for layers of buttered filo dough. If you like, use walnuts in place of the pecans, Roquefort in place of the Gorgonzola, and pears in place of the apples.

MAKES 24 PIECES, SERVES: 8–12

❋ Preheat an oven to 350°F (180°C). Lightly butter a large baking sheet. In a small, dry frying pan over low heat, toast the pecans, stirring continuously, until light golden brown and fragrant, about 8 minutes. Transfer to a plate and set aside.

❋ In a bowl, combine the apple, cheese, and flour and toss to mix well. Place a damp kitchen towel over the stack of filo to prevent the sheets from drying out.

❋ Lay a large sheet of waxed paper on a work surface. Place a filo sheet on top. Using a wide pastry brush, coat with a thin film of the melted butter. Top with a second filo sheet and then a third one, buttering each sheet.

❋ Sprinkle the buttered filo evenly with half of the pecans, then scatter half of the apple-cheese mixture over the nuts, distributing it as evenly as possible. Add a grinding of pepper. Top with 3 more filo sheets, brushing each one evenly with the butter.

❋ Starting from a long side, carefully roll up the filo layers as tightly as possible. Slide the roll onto the prepared baking sheet. Repeat with the remaining ingredients to make a second roll. Using a sharp, thin-bladed knife, cut about three-fourths of the way through the rolls at 1-inch (2.5-cm) intervals. This will make them easier to cut and serve after they are baked.

❋ Bake until golden, about 25 minutes. Remove from the oven and let cool completely on the baking sheet. Carefully slide the rolls onto a cutting board and finish cutting into pieces.

❋ Arrange the pieces, cut sides up, on a platter. Serve immediately.

NUTRITIONAL ANALYSIS PER PIECE: Calories 117 (Kilojoules 491); Protein 2 g; Carbohydrates 7 g; Total Fat 9 g; Saturated Fat 4 g; Cholesterol 15 mg; Sodium 112 mg; Dietary Fiber 0 g

Arugula and Orange Salad with Pomegranate–White Wine Vinaigrette

PREP TIME: 30 MINUTES

INGREDIENTS

FOR THE VINAIGRETTE

1 pomegranate

⅓ cup (3 fl oz/80 ml) extra-virgin olive oil

2 tablespoons white wine vinegar or raspberry vinegar

1 teaspoon sugar

½ teaspoon salt

ground pepper to taste

2 large navel oranges

3 bunches arugula (rocket), tough stems removed

1 small red (Spanish) onion, cut crosswise into thin rings

MAKE-AHEAD TIP: To save time the day of serving, remove the seeds from the pomegranate up to 2 days in advance. Store in the refrigerator in an airtight container. Do not extract the juice until 1–2 hours before making the vinaigrette.

Perfect for holiday entertaining, this salad features the traditional colors of Christmas. It also allows you to make good use of your fancy vinegars. Champagne vinegar, fruit-flavored vinegar, or white wine vinegar will work with the sweet and tart taste of the pomegranate and oranges.

SERVES 6

❀ To make the vinaigrette, carefully remove the skin from the pomegranate. Working over a sieve placed over a bowl to catch the juices, peel away the thick membrane from the pomegranate seeds and allow the loosened seeds to collect in the sieve. Measure ⅓ cup (1½ oz/45 g) of the seeds and reserve for garnish. Press on the remaining seeds with the back of a spoon to release about 2 tablespoons juice. Discard the crushed seeds.

❀ Add the olive oil, vinegar, sugar, salt, and pepper to the pomegranate juice. Whisk until blended.

❀ Using a small, sharp knife, cut a slice off the top and bottom of each orange to expose the flesh. Place each orange upright on a cutting board and thickly slice off the peel in strips, following the contour of the orange to expose the flesh. Holding the orange over a large bowl, cut along either side of each section, letting the section drop into the bowl. Add the arugula and red onion, separating the onion slices into rings. Drizzle the dressing over the arugula mixture, then toss to coat evenly.

❀ Divide the salad among individual plates, distributing the orange sections evenly. Garnish with the reserved pomegranate seeds. Serve at once.

NUTRITIONAL ANALYSIS PER SERVING: Calories 167 (Kilojoules 701); Protein 2 g; Carbohydrates 15 g; Total Fat 13 g; Saturated Fat 2 g; Cholesterol 0 mg; Sodium 204 mg; Dietary Fiber 2 g

Acorn Squash and Sweet Potato Soup with Walnut-Parsley Pesto

PREP TIME: 30 MINUTES

COOKING TIME: 1¼ HOURS

INGREDIENTS

1 large sweet onion such as Vidalia, halved and sliced

4 cloves garlic, coarsely chopped

2 tablespoons unsalted butter, cut into small pieces

1½ teaspoons salt, plus salt to taste

freshly ground pepper to taste

2 large acorn squashes, about 2 lb (1 kg) each, halved lengthwise and seeds and fibers removed

2 large sweet potatoes, about 1½ lb (750 g) total weight, peeled and sliced

FOR THE PESTO

½ cup (2 oz/60 g) walnuts

1 cup (1 oz/30 g) loosely packed fresh flat-leaf (Italian) parsley leaves with tender stems

1 clove garlic, coarsely chopped

½ teaspoon salt

⅔ cup (5 fl oz/160 ml) extra-virgin olive oil

¼ cup (1 oz/30 g) grated Parmesan cheese

4 cups (32 fl oz/1 l) reduced-sodium chicken broth

1½ cups (12 fl oz/375 ml) half-and-half (half cream) or heavy (double) cream, at room temperature

Your guests will be impressed when you serve this bright orange soup garnished with an emerald green swirl of parsley pesto. Roasting the acorn squashes and sweet potatoes helps to concentrate their flavors and gives this creamy soup an especially rich, robust taste.

SERVES 6–8

❊ Preheat an oven to 400°F (200°C). Spread the onion slices and garlic in a large roasting pan. Dot with the butter and sprinkle with ½ teaspoon of the salt and a grinding of pepper. Place the squashes and sweet potatoes, cut sides down, on top. Cover with aluminum foil. Bake until fork tender, about 1 hour. Uncover and let cool.

❊ To make the pesto, reduce the oven temperature to 350°F (180°C). Spread the walnuts on a baking sheet and toast in the oven, stirring once, until golden and fragrant, about 15 minutes. Remove from the oven and let cool slightly. In a food processor, combine the toasted walnuts, parsley, garlic, and salt and process until very finely chopped. With the motor running, add the olive oil in a slow, steady stream, processing until smooth and thick. Add the Parmesan and process until blended. You should have about ¾ cup (6 fl oz/180 ml).

❊ Remove the squash flesh from the shells and pass through a food mill placed over a large saucepan. Then pass the onion, garlic, sweet potatoes, and any juices in the roasting pan though the food mill into the saucepan. (Alternatively, working in batches, purée in a food processor, then pass the purée through a fine-mesh sieve into a large saucepan.) Add the broth and half-and-half or heavy cream and place over low heat. Bring to a simmer, stirring occasionally. Add the remaining 1 teaspoon salt, or more to taste, and a generous grinding of pepper. Do not allow to boil or the cream may curdle.

❊ Ladle the soup into warmed shallow bowls. Add 1½ teaspoons pesto to each bowl, forming a swirl in the surface of the soup. Serve at once. Pass any remaining pesto at the table.

NUTRITIONAL ANALYSIS PER SERVING: Calories 599 (Kilojoules 2,516); Protein 10 g; Carbohydrates 61 g; Total Fat 37 g; Saturated Fat 10 g; Cholesterol 31 mg; Sodium 1,111 mg; Dietary Fiber 12 g

Pan-Roasted Portobello Mushrooms with Three-Herb Gremolata

PREP TIME: 20 MINUTES

COOKING TIME: 35 MINUTES

INGREDIENTS

4 large fresh portobello mushrooms, about ¼ lb (125 g) each, brushed clean and stem ends trimmed

½ cup (4 fl oz/120 ml) extra-virgin olive oil

salt and ground pepper to taste

½ cup (¾ oz/20 g) firmly packed fresh flat-leaf (Italian) parsley

1 tablespoon fresh thyme leaves, plus sprigs for garnish

1 teaspoon fresh rosemary leaves

2 cloves garlic, finely chopped

2 teaspoons finely chopped lemon zest, plus zest strips for garnish (optional)

⅓ cup (2 oz/60 g) finely chopped yellow onion

1 small head radicchio, cored and quartered lengthwise

1 teaspoon red wine vinegar

PREP TIP: Remove the lemon zest with a zester, avoiding the bitter white pith. Or use a vegetable peeler, removing the zest in a wide strip, and then finely chop it.

Beautiful, large portobello mushrooms are juicy and meaty when oven roasted, making an impressive holiday appetizer.

SERVES 4

❋ Preheat an oven to 400°F (200°C).

❋ Remove the stems from the mushrooms and finely chop the stems; set aside. Arrange the mushroom caps, rounded sides up, in a single layer in a large baking dish. Brush with ¼ cup (2 fl oz/60 ml) of the olive oil and sprinkle with salt and pepper. Bake until lightly browned, about 15 minutes.

❋ Meanwhile, finely chop together the parsley, thyme leaves, rosemary, garlic, and the 2 teaspoons lemon zest. Combine in a bowl with the onion and reserved mushroom stems. In another bowl, combine the radicchio with cold water to cover and let soak for 20–30 minutes to crisp.

❋ Remove the baking dish from the oven. Reduce the oven temperature to 350°F (180°C). Turn the mushrooms over. Sprinkle with salt and pepper. Spoon the herb mixture into the center of the mushrooms, mounding it slightly. Drizzle with 2 tablespoons of the remaining oil.

❋ Continue to bake until the mushrooms are very tender and the filling is softened, 10–15 minutes. Using a wide spatula, press the filling down into the gills of the mushrooms, then turn the mushrooms over again. Bake until soft and tender, about 5 minutes longer.

❋ Meanwhile, drain the radicchio well, then thinly slice. In a large sauté pan over medium heat, warm the remaining 2 tablespoons olive oil. Add the radicchio and quickly toss and stir until heated through but still crisp, about 2 minutes. Remove from the heat, sprinkle with the vinegar, season with salt and pepper, and toss to blend.

❋ Divide the radicchio evenly among individual plates. Place a portobello mushroom, smooth side up, on each mound of radicchio. Sprinkle with any bits left in the pan. Garnish with the thyme sprigs and strips of lemon zest, if using, and serve immediately.

NUTRITIONAL ANALYSIS PER SERVING: Calories 286 (Kilojoules 1,201); Protein 3 g; Carbohydrates 9 g; Total Fat 29 g; Saturated Fat 4 g; Cholesterol 0 mg; Sodium 14 mg; Dietary Fiber 2 g

Cornmeal-Crusted Oysters with Sour Cream and Caviar

Oysters are a delicacy traditionally enjoyed with a glass of sparkling wine—what better way to kick off a holiday feast? Fried oysters are a great alternative to raw for people who love oysters but prefer them cooked. Bread the oysters ahead of time and quickly fry just before serving. The sour cream and black caviar add a deluxe touch.

PREP TIME: 20 MINUTES

COOKING TIME: 15 MINUTES

INGREDIENTS

24 oysters, shucked, with 4–6 shells reserved

½ cup (2½ oz/75 g) yellow cornmeal

½ cup (2½ oz/75 g) all-purpose (plain) flour

¾ teaspoon salt

½ teaspoon cayenne pepper

¼ teaspoon ground black pepper

2 eggs

vegetable oil for frying

1 cup (8 fl oz/250 ml) sour cream

2 oz (60 g) black caviar, or to taste

fresh flat-leaf (Italian) parsley sprigs

MAKE-AHEAD TIP: You can bread the oysters up to 1 hour ahead. Place on a tray or platter, then refrigerate until ready to quickly fry just before serving.

SERVES 4–6

✳ Preheat an oven to 200°F (95°C).

✳ Drain the oysters and blot on a double thickness of paper towels to remove excess moisture. On a sheet of waxed paper, combine the cornmeal, flour, salt, cayenne pepper, and black pepper. In a shallow bowl, whisk the eggs until blended.

✳ One at a time, roll the oysters in the cornmeal mixture, shaking off the excess. Dip them into the eggs and then roll them again in the cornmeal mixture to coat lightly. Place on a tray or platter, then refrigerate until ready to fry.

✳ Pour vegetable oil to a depth of 1 inch (2.5 cm) in a large frying pan and place over medium heat. To test if the oil is hot enough, drop a tiny crust of bread into it; it should sizzle upon contact. Add the oysters, 6–8 at a time, and fry, turning once, until golden, about 4 minutes. Using tongs or a slotted spoon, transfer to paper towels to drain. Keep warm until all are cooked. Repeat with the remaining oysters.

✳ To serve, spoon the sour cream into the reserved oyster shells, dividing it evenly, and top each with a small spoonful of caviar. Place a shell in the center of each individual plate. Surround with the hot oysters. Garnish with a parsley sprig.

NUTRITIONAL ANALYSIS PER SERVING: Calories 329 (Kilojoules 1,382); Protein 13 g; Carbohydrates 22 g; Total Fat 21 g; Saturated Fat 8 g; Cholesterol 209 mg; Sodium 528 mg; Dietary Fiber 1 g

Watercress, Pear, and Goat Cheese Salad with Sherry Vinaigrette

PREP TIME: 20 MINUTES

INGREDIENTS

3 firm but ripe Bartlett (Williams') pears

juice from ½ lemon

2 or 3 bunches watercress, long stems removed (about 8 cups/ 8 oz/250 g)

½ cup (2 oz/60 g) moist dried pitted sweet cherries

FOR THE VINAIGRETTE

6 tablespoons (3 fl oz/90 ml) extra-virgin olive oil

2 tablespoons sherry wine vinegar

½ teaspoon salt

ground pepper to taste

5 oz (155 g) semifirm mild-aged goat cheese, cut into small pieces

PREP TIP: The easiest way to core a pear is to first cut it in half and then use a rounded metal measuring teaspoon or melon baller to scoop out the core.

If preferred, a mix of young, tender salad greens can be used in place of the watercress, while Bosc pears can stand in for the Bartletts. And, if you like, a cow's milk cheese such as a mild Gorgonzola dolcelatte can replace the goat cheese.

SERVES 6

❁ Peel, halve, and core the pears, then cut each half into 4 wedges. As the pears are cut, place them in a large bowl and sprinkle with the lemon juice. Add the watercress and cherries.

❁ To make the vinaigrette, in a small bowl, whisk together the olive oil, sherry vinegar, salt, and pepper until blended.

❁ Drizzle the vinaigrette over the watercress mixture, then toss to coat evenly. Divide the salad evenly among individual plates. Add the goat cheese to the salads, distributing it evenly. Serve immediately.

NUTRITIONAL ANALYSIS PER SERVING: Calories 294 (Kilojoules 1,235); Protein 7 g; Carbohydrates 21 g; Total Fat 22 g; Saturated Fat 7 g; Cholesterol 22 mg; Sodium 310 mg; Dietary Fiber 3 g

Layered Vegetable Terrine with Mustard Vinaigrette

PREP TIME: 40 MINUTES

COOKING TIME: 1¼ HOURS,
PLUS 30 MINUTES FOR
STANDING

INGREDIENTS

FOR THE TERRINE

6 thin slices peeled Asian eggplant
(aubergine)

2 large red bell peppers (capsicums),
halved lengthwise and seeded

2 fresh portobello mushrooms,
brushed clean and thinly sliced

1 yellow summer squash, cut lengthwise into 3 or 4 slices

½ cup (4 fl oz/125 ml) extra-virgin
olive oil

2 cloves garlic, finely chopped

2 leeks, halved lengthwise

2 tablespoons water

½ lb (250 g) spinach, stemmed

salt and ground pepper to taste

½ cup (½ oz/15 g) loosely packed
fresh basil leaves, torn into pieces,
plus leaves for garnish (optional)

¼ lb (125 g) mozzarella cheese,
thinly sliced

FOR THE VINAIGRETTE

3 tablespoons red wine vinegar

1 tablespoon balsamic vinegar

1 clove garlic, finely chopped

1 teaspoon Dijon mustard

1 teaspoon dried thyme

salt and ground pepper to taste

⅔ cup (5 fl oz/160 ml) extra-virgin
olive oil

SERVES 8

❋ Preheat an oven to 400°F (200°C). Lightly oil 2 large baking sheets. Arrange the eggplant and bell peppers, cut sides down, on 1 baking sheet. Arrange the mushrooms and squash on the second baking sheet. In a small bowl, combine the oil and garlic and brush lightly over the vegetables. Roast the mushrooms and squash until lightly browned on the bottoms, about 15 minutes. Turn and roast the other side, about 10 minutes longer. At the same time, roast the eggplant and peppers until browned on one side, about 25 minutes. Turn and brown the other side, about 20 minutes longer. Remove all the vegetables from the oven. Transfer the peppers to a work surface, drape loosely with aluminum foil, and let cool, then peel off the charred skin. Let all the vegetables cool.

❋ Meanwhile, arrange the leeks in a baking dish. Add the water and drizzle with a little of the remaining oil-garlic mixture. Cover tightly and bake until very tender, 25–30 minutes. Remove from the oven and let cool. Place the spinach on a steamer rack over simmering water, cover, and steam until wilted, about 2 minutes. Transfer to a sieve and press down to extract the moisture. Chop coarsely.

❋ Reduce the oven temperature to 350°F (180°C). Lightly brush a 1½-qt (1.5-l) glass loaf dish with any remaining oil-garlic mixture. Sprinkle all of the vegetables with salt and pepper. Arrange the pepper halves in the bottom of the prepared dish, cut sides up. Arrange the squash slices on top in a single layer. Sprinkle with half of the torn basil, top with the spinach, and then with the cheese. Arrange the mushrooms in a layer, and top with the leeks. Sprinkle with the remaining basil. Top with the eggplant slices, slightly overlapping them. Cover with foil and press down to compact the vegetables. Bake until heated through, about 30 minutes. Remove from the oven but do not uncover. Let stand for about 30 minutes before serving.

❋ To make the vinaigrette, in a bowl, whisk together the vinegars, garlic, mustard, thyme, salt, and pepper. Slowly whisk in the oil.

❋ Loosen the sides of the terrine, then unmold onto a cutting board. Cut into thick slices and serve atop a spoonful of vinaigrette. Garnish with basil, if desired. Pass the remaining vinaigrette at the table.

NUTRITIONAL ANALYSIS PER SERVING: Calories 376 (Kilojoules 1,579); Protein 5 g; Carbohydrates 10 g; Total Fat 37 g; Saturated Fat 7 g; Cholesterol 11 mg; Sodium 237 mg; Dietary Fiber 2 g

Roasted Tomato Soup with Tiny Meatballs and Rice

PREP TIME: 30 MINUTES,
PLUS 1 HOUR FOR CHILLING

COOKING TIME: 1¼ HOURS

INGREDIENTS

4 lb (2 kg) ripe tomatoes, halved crosswise

1 large sweet onion such as Vidalia, cut into wedges

½ cup (4 fl oz/125 ml) extra-virgin olive oil

2 fresh thyme sprigs

1 fresh rosemary sprig

¾ cup (1½ oz/45 g) coarse fresh bread crumbs

1½ cups (12 fl oz/375 ml) water

½ lb (250 g) ground (minced) veal, turkey, or lean pork

1 egg

¼ cup (1 oz/30 g) grated Parmesan cheese

1 tablespoon torn fresh sage leaves

1 teaspoon salt, plus salt to taste

ground pepper to taste

⅓ cup (2 oz/60 g) Arborio rice

about 2 cups (16 fl oz/500 ml) beef or vegetable broth

⅓ cup (½ oz/15 g) firmly packed fresh flat-leaf (Italian) parsley leaves

1 orange zest strip, 3 inches (7.5 cm) long and ½ inch (12 mm) wide

1 clove garlic

Intensely flavored roasted tomatoes and extra-virgin olive oil give this soup a wonderfully fruity flavor. The tomato base can be made up to 1 week in advance and frozen.

SERVES 6–8

❋ Preheat an oven to 400°F (200°C). Arrange the tomato and onion pieces, cut sides down, on a large baking sheet. Drizzle with the olive oil and lay the thyme and rosemary sprigs on top. Roast until the tomatoes begin to char and the onions are tender, about 45 minutes. Remove from the oven and let cool slightly.

❋ Meanwhile, make the meatballs: In a bowl, combine the bread crumbs and ½ cup (4 fl oz/125 ml) of the water. Let soften, about 5 minutes. Add the meat, egg, cheese, sage, 1 teaspoon of the salt, and pepper. Using your hands, mix well. Cover and chill for 1 hour.

❋ While the meat is chilling, cook the rice: In a heavy saucepan over high heat, bring the remaining 1 cup (8 fl oz/250 ml) water to a boil. Add the rice, reduce the heat to low, cover, and cook until the rice is tender and all the water has been absorbed, about 15 minutes.

❋ Pass the tomatoes, onion, and juices through a food mill placed over a large bowl. Discard the solids. (Alternatively, purée in a food processor, then pass the purée through a fine-mesh sieve into a large bowl.) Measure the tomato mixture; there should be about 6 cups (48 fl oz/1.5 l). Add enough meat or vegetable broth to measure 8 cups (64 fl oz/2 l) total. Transfer to a large saucepan and place over medium heat. Bring to a simmer, reduce the heat to very low, and cover.

❋ Shape the meat mixture into tiny balls each about ¾ inch (2 cm) in diameter. There should be about 25 meatballs. Slip the meatballs into the broth, re-cover, raise the heat to low, and simmer gently until cooked through, about 5 minutes. Add the rice and heat through. Season with salt and pepper. While the rice is heating, on a cutting board, finely chop together the parsley, orange zest, and garlic.

❋ Ladle the soup into warmed bowls, distributing the meatballs evenly. Sprinkle with a little of the parsley mixture and serve immediately.

NUTRITIONAL ANALYSIS PER SERVING: Calories 333 (Kilojoules 1,399); Protein 13 g; Carbohydrates 26 g; Total Fat 21 g; Saturated Fat 4 g; Cholesterol 60 mg; Sodium 891 mg; Dietary Fiber 4 g

Celery Root and Carrot Salad with Creamy Dressing

PREP TIME: 25 MINUTES, PLUS
1 HOUR FOR MARINATING

INGREDIENTS

FOR THE DRESSING

½ cup (4 fl oz/125 ml) pure olive oil or 2 tablespoons pure olive oil and 6 tablespoons (3 fl oz/90 ml) extra-virgin olive oil

¼ cup (2 fl oz/60 ml) heavy (double) cream

2 tablespoons Dijon mustard

2 tablespoons tarragon vinegar

¾ teaspoon salt

ground pepper to taste

1 large celery root, about 1½ lb (750 g)

½ cup (2 oz/60 g) coarsely shredded carrot

6 large butter (Boston) lettuce leaves

1 tablespoon capers, rinsed and well drained

fresh tarragon sprigs (optional)

PREP TIP: Celery root darkens quickly once the flesh is exposed to air. To discourage discoloring, immerse cut celery root in a bowl of water mixed with a tablespoon or so of lemon juice or vinegar until ready to coat with the dressing.

This crisp, refreshing salad is best made a day ahead so that the flavors have a chance to develop fully. Celery root is a rather ungainly vegetable with a rough exterior that must be peeled away with a sharp knife. The flavor is similar to that of stalk celery. This recipe is an adaptation of the classic French salad, *céleri-rave rémoulade.*

SERVES 6

❈ To make the dressing, in a large nonaluminum bowl, combine the olive oil, cream, mustard, vinegar, salt, and pepper. Whisk until blended.

❈ Using a sharp knife, peel away the tough skin from the celery root. Using a mandoline or the knife, cut into thin julienne strips about 3 inches (7.5 cm) long. Immediately add to the dressing and turn to coat well. Work quickly, as the flesh begins to discolor as soon as it is exposed to the air. Add the shredded carrot and mix well. Cover and refrigerate for at least 1 hour or for as long as overnight before serving. (If the salad becomes very cold, let stand at room temperature for 15 minutes before serving.)

❈ To serve, arrange a lettuce leaf on each individual plate. Divide the celery root mixture evenly among the leaves. Sprinkle each salad with a few capers. Garnish with tarragon sprigs, if using. Serve at once.

NUTRITIONAL ANALYSIS PER SERVING: Calories 244 (Kilojoules 1,025); Protein 2 g; Carbohydrates 11 g; Total Fat 22 g; Saturated Fat 5 g; Cholesterol 14 mg; Sodium 482 mg; Dietary Fiber 0 g

Three-Mushroom Chowder with Roasted Red Pepper Purée

PREP TIME: 40 MINUTES

COOKING TIME: 50 MINUTES

INGREDIENTS

FOR THE ROASTED RED PEPPER PUREE

2 red bell peppers (capsicums)

6 tablespoons (3 fl oz/90 ml) heavy
(double) cream

2 teaspoons tomato paste

½ teaspoon salt, or to taste

⅛ teaspoon cayenne pepper, or
to taste

FOR THE MUSHROOM CHOWDER

2 cups (16 fl oz/500 ml) reduced-
sodium chicken broth

½ cup (1 oz/30 g) dried porcini
mushrooms

6 tablespoons (3 oz/90 g) unsalted
butter

½ cup (2½ oz/75 g) finely chopped
yellow onion

¾ lb (375 g) fresh white button mushrooms, brushed clean and finely
chopped

¾ lb (375 g) fresh cremini mushrooms,
brushed clean and finely chopped

6 tablespoons (2 oz/60 g) all-purpose
(plain) flour

½ teaspoon salt, plus salt to taste

freshly ground black pepper to taste

4 cups (32 fl oz/1 l) milk

1 cup (8 fl oz/250 ml) heavy
(double) cream

2–3 tablespoons dry sherry

Mushrooms, especially the prized porcini of Italy, add an especially festive note to your holiday table. The dried porcini give this soup its intense mushroom taste.

SERVES 6

❋ To make the pepper purée, preheat a broiler (griller). Place the peppers on a baking sheet lined with aluminum foil. Broil (grill), turning as needed, until the skins blacken and blister. Remove from the broiler, wrap the peppers loosely with the foil, and let cool for 10 minutes. Working over the foil, peel away the skins. Reserve the juices from the foil. (You should have about 1 tablespoon.) Cut the peppers in half lengthwise and remove the stems, seeds, and ribs. Cut the peppers into pieces and place in a food processor with the reserved juices, the cream, tomato paste, salt, and cayenne pepper and process until smooth. You should have about ¾ cup (6 fl oz/180 ml). Set aside.

❋ Meanwhile, begin making the chowder: in a small saucepan, combine the broth and porcini and bring to a boil. Cover, remove from the heat, and then let stand for 20 minutes. Pour through a fine-mesh sieve lined with dampened cheesecloth (muslin) placed over a small bowl; reserve the liquid. If the porcini feel gritty, rinse with cold water. Squeeze dry and chop finely. Set aside.

❋ In a large saucepan over medium-low heat, melt the butter. Add the onion and sauté until tender but not browned, about 5 minutes. Increase the heat to medium and add the fresh mushrooms. Cook, stirring, until tender, about 10 minutes. Stir in the reserved chopped porcini. Add the flour, ½ teaspoon salt, and a grinding of black pepper, and stir until thoroughly blended. Cook, stirring, for 3 minutes. Gradually add the milk and reserved porcini broth. Cook, stirring, until the mixture boils and thickens, about 10 minutes. Reduce the heat to very low and cook, uncovered, to blend the flavors, about 10 minutes longer; do not allow to boil. Add the cream and cook until very hot but not boiling. Stir in the sherry to taste and season with salt and black pepper.

❋ Ladle into warmed bowls. Spoon a generous tablespoonful of the red pepper purée into each bowl. Serve immediately.

NUTRITIONAL ANALYSIS PER SERVING: Calories 497 (Kilojoules 2,087); Protein 12 g; Carbohydrates 27 g; Total Fat 38 g; Saturated Fat 23 g; Cholesterol 129 mg; Sodium 695 mg; Dietary Fiber 4 g

Roasted Beet and Wilted Beet Greens Salad with Orange Vinaigrette

PREP TIME: 15 MINUTES

COOKING TIME: 55 MINUTES,
PLUS 1 HOUR FOR COOLING

INGREDIENTS

6 bunches beets with leafy green tops, about 3 lb (1.5 kg) total

1 teaspoon salt

FOR THE VINAIGRETTE

⅓ cup (3 fl oz/80 ml) extra-virgin olive oil

3 tablespoons red wine vinegar

2 teaspoons finely grated or chopped orange zest

salt and ground pepper to taste

½ sweet onion such as Vidalia, cut crosswise into thin slices

6 thin navel orange slices, halved

snipped fresh chives (optional)

MAKE-AHEAD TIP: The beets can be cooked up to 3 days ahead and refrigerated still tightly wrapped in the foil. Unwrap and peel the skins from the beets just before serving.

If the beet leaves are not fresh and tender, discard them and substitute 2 or 3 bunches of arugula (rocket). Rinse the arugula and trim away the tough stems. It is not necessary to cook the arugula leaves. Simply toss with the dressing and top with the sliced beets.

SERVES 6

⊛ Preheat an oven to 350°F (180°C). Trim off the beet greens, leaving about ½ inch (12 mm) of the stems intact; reserve the leaves. Rinse the beets well but do not peel. Wrap each beet tightly in a piece of heavy-duty aluminum foil; double fold the edges so the juices won't leak out. Place directly on the center oven rack. Bake until tender when pierced with a skewer, 45–55 minutes.

⊛ Meanwhile, trim the long stems from the beet greens and reserve only the leaves that are free of blemishes, discarding the others. Rinse thoroughly and dry well. Gather the leaves together and cut crosswise into strips 1 inch (2.5 cm) wide.

⊛ Half fill a saucepan with water and bring to a boil over high heat. Add the beet greens and salt and cook, uncovered, until the greens are tender, about 8 minutes. Drain well and set aside.

⊛ When the beets are ready, remove from the oven and leave wrapped in the foil until cool enough to handle, about 1 hour. Then carefully remove the foil and rub off the skins. If there are beet juices in the foil, place the juices in a small bowl.

⊛ To make the vinaigrette, add the olive oil, vinegar, orange zest, salt, and pepper to any beet juices in the small bowl. Whisk to blend.

⊛ Cut the beets into wedges. In a large bowl, combine the beets, onion, cooked beet greens, and dressing. Toss to mix.

⊛ Divide the salad among individual plates. Garnish each salad with 2 orange slice halves and snipped fresh chives, if using. Serve at once.

NUTRITIONAL ANALYSIS PER SERVING: Calories 174 (Kilojoules 731); Protein 3 g; Carbohydrates 16 g; Total Fat 13 g; Saturated Fat 2 g; Cholesterol 0 mg; Sodium 273 mg; Dietary Fiber 2 g

Seafood Bisque

PREP TIME: 45 MINUTES

COOKING TIME: 1 HOUR

INGREDIENTS

8 cups (64 fl oz/2 l) water

2 fresh thyme sprigs or 1 teaspoon dried thyme

2 fresh tarragon sprigs or 1 teaspoon dried tarragon

1 large sweet onion such as Vidalia, halved

1 bay leaf

1 leafy celery stalk top

1 teaspoon salt, plus salt to taste

1 live lobster, about 1½ lb (750 g)

½ lb (250 g) large shrimp (prawns) in the shell

¼ cup (2 oz/60 g) unsalted butter, at room temperature

¼ cup (1½ oz/ 45 g) all-purpose (plain) flour

2 cups (16 fl oz/500 ml) heavy (double) cream

1 tablespoon tomato paste

ground white pepper to taste

½ lb (250 g) bay scallops

fresh thyme or tarragon sprigs

MAKE-AHEAD TIP: You can make this soup up to two days in advance and reheat, stirring gently, over low heat.

This rich bisque, thick with lobster, shrimp, and bay scallops, should be served in small bowls or cups.

SERVES 6

❀ In a large, wide saucepan over medium heat, combine the water, thyme, tarragon, onion, bay leaf, celery top, and 1 teaspoon salt. Bring to a boil, cover, reduce the heat to low, and simmer to blend the flavors, about 10 minutes. Uncover, raise the heat to high, and bring back to a boil. Add the lobster, cover, reduce the heat to medium-high, and cook for 8 minutes. Uncover, add the shrimp, re-cover, and cook until the shrimp turn pink, about 4 minutes.

❀ Using tongs, transfer the lobster to a platter to cool. Place a colander over a large bowl and strain the contents of the saucepan. Return the broth to the saucepan. Pick out the shrimp and place on the platter with the lobster. Discard the other solids.

❀ Lay the cooled lobster, right side up, on a cutting board. Insert a knife where the body meets the tail and cut the tail in half lengthwise. Turn the lobster and continue the cut toward the head, cutting the lobster into 2 pieces. Remove the organs and discard. Remove the meat from the body. Using a mallet, crack the claws and knuckles and remove the meat. Peel the shrimp. Work over the platter as much as possible so that you can save all the juices and the shells. Cut the lobster and shrimp into ½-inch (12-mm) pieces. Set aside. Return the shells and juices to the broth, bring to a simmer, cover, reduce the heat to low, and cook until the broth is fragrant, about 30 minutes. Let cool slightly, then strain into a bowl.

❀ In a saucepan over medium heat, melt the butter. Stir in the flour and cook, stirring, until blended, about 3 minutes. Gradually whisk in the broth and bring to a boil. Reduce the heat to low and gradually stir in the cream. Add the tomato paste, salt, white pepper, and the reserved lobster and shrimp. Stir to blend, then heat through. Add the scallops and cook, stirring, until opaque and tender, about 1 minute. Taste and adjust the seasonings.

❀ Ladle into warmed bowls, garnish with the herb sprigs, and serve.

NUTRITIONAL ANALYSIS PER SERVING: Calories 486 (Kilojoules 2,041); Protein 21 g; Carbohydrates 15 g; Total Fat 38 g; Saturated Fat 23 g; Cholesterol 207 mg; Sodium 651 mg; Dietary Fiber 1 g

Pan-Seared Scallops with Apple-Onion Marmalade and Bacon

PREP TIME: 25 MINUTES

COOKING TIME: 1 HOUR

INGREDIENTS

FOR THE MARMALADE

¼ cup (2 fl oz/60 ml) olive oil

2 large sweet onions such as Vidalia, cut through the stem end into thin wedges

2 large Golden Delicious or other baking apples, peeled, cored, and cut into thin wedges

½ teaspoon cumin seeds

2 teaspoons apple cider vinegar, or more to taste

¾ teaspoon salt

ground pepper to taste

6 slices lean bacon

18 large sea scallops, about 1½ lb (750 g) total weight, patted dry

salt and ground pepper to taste

1 cup (8 fl oz/250 ml) apple cider

MAKE-AHEAD TIP: You can make the marmalade 2 or 3 days ahead. Reheat gently in a frying pan just before serving.

The sophisticated flavors of this lovely scallop starter will surely impress your guests. Yet it's very simple to prepare. Look for the largest sea scallops you can find as they will remain juicy and tender once seared.

SERVES 6

❊ To make the marmalade, in a large frying pan over medium to medium-low heat, warm the olive oil. Add the onions and cook, stirring often, until they begin to soften, about 15 minutes. Stir in the apples and cumin seeds. Cook, stirring, until the onions are golden and the apples soften, about 30 minutes longer. Add the cider vinegar, salt, and pepper and remove from the heat. You should have about 3 cups (scant 2 lb/1 kg). Set aside in the pan.

❊ In another large frying pan over medium-high heat, fry the bacon until crisp, 3–5 minutes. Using tongs or a slotted spatula, transfer to paper towels to drain. Discard all but about 1 tablespoon (a light coating) of the bacon drippings from the pan.

❊ Sprinkle the scallops lightly with salt and pepper. Return the frying pan to medium-high heat. When the pan is hot, add the scallops a few at a time and cook, turning once, until lightly browned on both sides, about 1 minute on each side. Transfer to a plate and keep warm while you cook the remaining scallops. When all the scallops are cooked, add the apple cider to the pan and boil until reduced by half, about 5 minutes. Pour any juices that have collected on the scallop plate into the frying pan. Remove from the heat.

❊ Meanwhile, reheat the marmalade over medium-low heat until heated through. Spread about ½ cup (5 oz/155 g) of the marmalade on each individual plate. Top each portion with 3 scallops, then drizzle with about 1 tablespoon of the cider sauce. Crumble the bacon over the scallops, dividing it evenly. Serve warm.

NUTRITIONAL ANALYSIS PER SERVING: Calories 326 (Kilojoules 1,369); Protein 23 g; Carbohydrates 25 g; Total Fat 15 g; Saturated Fat 3 g; Cholesterol 44 mg; Sodium 599 mg; Dietary Fiber 3 g

Standing Rib Roast with Jerusalem Artichokes and Potatoes

PREP TIME: 30 MINUTES,
PLUS 30 MINUTES FOR
MARINATING

COOKING TIME: 2½ HOURS

INGREDIENTS

2 teaspoons dried rosemary

1 teaspoon dried thyme

2 cloves garlic, lightly crushed

1 teaspoon coarse salt, plus salt
to taste

½ teaspoon ground pepper, plus
pepper to taste

3-rib standing rib roast, about 8½ lb
(4.25 kg)

10 –12 Yukon Gold or other yellow-
fleshed potatoes (2½–3 lb/
1.25–1.5 kg total weight),
peeled and halved

1 lb (500 g) shallots (about 24),
peeled but left whole

2 lb (1 kg) Jerusalem artichokes,
unpeeled

1 cup (8 fl oz/250 ml) full-bodied
red wine such as Cabernet
Sauvignon or Merlot

1 cup (8 fl oz/250 ml) beef broth

COOKING TIP: Use a heavy, good-
quality roasting pan so that the meat
juices will not burn on the pan bottom.

A standing rib roast is one of the most celebratory of all holiday dishes. Here, vegetables are roasted alongside in the same pan.

SERVES 12–14

❋ In a small bowl, stir together the rosemary, thyme, garlic, 1 teaspoon coarse salt, and ½ teaspoon pepper. Place the rib roast, rib side down, in a large roasting pan. Rub half of the herb mixture on the top and sides of the roast. Let stand at room temperature for 30 minutes. Preheat an oven to 475°F (245°C).

❋ Roast for 20 minutes. Remove from the oven and, using a spoon or bulb baster, transfer most of the rendered fat to a measuring pitcher; set aside. Reduce the oven temperature to 350°F (180°C) and continue to roast for 30 minutes.

❋ Meanwhile, in a large bowl, toss together the potatoes, shallots, and about ¼ cup (2 fl oz/60 ml) of the reserved fat. (Discard the remaining fat.) Sprinkle with salt and pepper.

❋ When the meat has roasted for 50 minutes, arrange the potatoes and shallots around it in the pan and continue to roast for 30 minutes. Add the Jerusalem artichokes, and sprinkle all the vegetables with the remaining herb mixture. Continue to roast until an instant-read ther-mometer inserted into the thickest part of the roast away from the bone registers 125°–130°F (52°–54°C) for medium-rare and the vegeta-bles are tender, 30–45 minutes longer.

❋ Transfer the roast to a warmed platter. Cover with aluminum foil and let stand for 20 minutes. Transfer the vegetables to a dish and keep warm. Pour the pan juices into a cup and spoon off most of the fat. Return the juices to the pan, along with the wine and broth. Place over medium-high heat, bring to a boil, and deglaze the pan, stirring to dislodge any browned bits from the pan bottom. Continue to cook until reduced by one-half, about 15 minutes. Pour through a sieve into a small pitcher. Season to taste with salt and pepper.

❋ Carve the meat across the grain into slices. Pour the juices over the meat. Pass the vegetables at the table.

NUTRITIONAL ANALYSIS PER SERVING: Calories 950 (Kilojoules 3,990); Protein 47 g; Carbohydrates 31 g; Total Fat 70 g; Saturated Fat 29 g; Cholesterol 174 mg; Sodium 311 mg; Dietary Fiber 2 g

Apple-Stuffed Pork Loin with Cider Sauce

SERVES 8

PREP TIME: 30 MINUTES

COOKING TIME: 1½ HOURS

INGREDIENTS

FOR THE STUFFING

2 tablespoons olive oil

1½ cups (6 oz/185 g) chopped Golden Delicious or other baking apple

1 cup (4 oz/125 g) chopped yellow onion

1 clove garlic, finely chopped

½ cup (1½ oz/45 g) finely chopped dried apples or ½ cup (3 oz/90 g) finely chopped dried apricots

¼ cup (1½ oz/45 g) raisins

¼ teaspoon dried thyme

salt and ground pepper to taste

½ cup (4 fl oz/125 ml) apple cider

1 boneless pork loin, 2½ lb (1.25 kg)

¼ teaspoon dried thyme

salt and ground pepper to taste

1 cup (8 fl oz/250 ml) apple cider, plus more as needed

2 teaspoons cornstarch (cornflour)

SERVING TIP: Add ¼ cup (1 oz/30 g) dried cranberries to the stuffing with the apple and serve Cranberry Relish (page 62) on the side. This roast is also good cold as part of a buffet. Slice the loin thin, but do not serve the cider sauce.

❋ To make the stuffing, in a large frying pan over medium-low heat, warm the olive oil. Add the apple and onion and sauté until golden, about 5 minutes. Stir in the garlic and cook for 1 minute. Add the dried apples or apricots, raisins, and thyme and season with salt and pepper. Add the apple cider and boil, stirring occasionally, until the cider is absorbed by the stuffing, about 5 minutes. Let cool slightly.

❋ Preheat an oven to 400°F (200°C). Have ready 4 pieces of kitchen string, each 18 inches (45 cm) long. Butterfly the pork loin by making a slit down its length, cutting just deep enough so that the loin opens up to lie flat like a book. Do not cut all the way through. Spoon the stuffing evenly onto the meat. Close up the loin and, using the strings, tie at even intervals so it assumes its original shape. Push in any stuffing that escapes from the ends. Sprinkle the surface with the ¼ teaspoon thyme and season with salt and pepper. Place in a baking pan and add ½ cup (4 fl oz/125 ml) of the cider to the pan.

❋ Roast the loin for 30 minutes. Baste with the pan juices and add the remaining ½ cup (4 fl oz/125 ml) cider to the pan. Continue to roast, basting at least twice with the pan juices at regular intervals, until the meat is firm to the touch and pale pink when cut in the thickest portion, or until an instant-read thermometer inserted into the thickest point registers 160°F (71°C), about 45 minutes longer.

❋ Transfer the loin to a cutting board and cover with a piece of aluminum foil. Scrape the pan bottom to dislodge any remaining bits, then pour the pan juices into a measuring pitcher and add additional cider as needed to measure 1½ cups (12 fl oz/375 ml) total. In a small saucepan, combine ¼ cup (2 fl oz/60 ml) of the pan juices and the cornstarch; stir until the cornstarch is dissolved. Add the remaining pan juices. Bring to a boil over medium heat and cook, stirring, until slightly thickened, about 5 minutes. Taste and adjust the seasonings. Pour into a warmed bowl.

❋ Cut the loin into slices and arrange on a warmed platter. Serve the hot cider sauce on the side.

NUTRITIONAL ANALYSIS PER SERVING: Calories 383 (Kilojoules 1,609); Protein 28 g; Carbohydrates 18 g; Total Fat 21 g; Saturated Fat 7 g; Cholesterol 89 mg; Sodium 78 mg; Dietary Fiber 1 g

Roasted Turkey with Barley Stuffing

PREP TIME: 30 MINUTES

COOKING TIME: 4½ HOURS

INGREDIENTS

FOR THE STUFFING

8 cups (64 fl oz/2 l) water

1 thick orange slice

1 cinnamon stick

1 leafy celery stalk top

1 carrot, halved

1 tablespoon salt

2 whole cloves

½ yellow onion, plus 2 cups (8 oz/ 250 g) chopped yellow onion

2 cups (1 lb/500 g) pearl barley

½ cup (4 oz/125 g) unsalted butter

1 cup (6 oz/185 g) dried apricot halves, quartered

1 cup (6 oz/185 g) pitted prunes, quartered

½ cup (3 oz/90 g) dark or golden raisins (sultanas)

1 cup (5 oz/155 g) coarsely chopped almonds

¼ cup (2 fl oz/60 ml) lemon juice

1 turkey, 12–14 lb (6–7 kg), giblets and neck removed

1 lemon, halved

salt and ground pepper to taste

4 tablespoons (2 oz/60 g) unsalted butter

SERVES 10–12

❋ To make the stuffing, in a wide saucepan, combine the water, orange slice, cinnamon stick, celery top, carrot, and salt. Stick the whole cloves into the onion half, add to the pan, and bring to a boil. Stir in the barley, cover, reduce the heat to low, and cook until the barley is plump and tender, about 55 minutes. Drain off any water left in the pan. Discard the vegetables and spices. Set the barley aside.

❋ In a large frying pan over medium heat, melt the butter. Add the chopped onion and cook, stirring often, until golden, about 10 minutes. Add the apricots, prunes, raisins, and almonds; stir to coat. Add the barley and cook, stirring, until heated through, about 10 minutes. Mix in the lemon juice and set aside to cool.

❋ Preheat an oven to 325°F (165°C). Rinse the turkey and pat dry with paper towels. Place the turkey, breast side up, on a rack in a large roasting pan or covered roaster. Squeeze the lemon juice inside and outside the turkey, then rub the skin with the lemon halves. Sprinkle with salt and pepper. Spoon about 1 cup (8 oz/250 g) of the stuffing into the neck cavity; pull the skin over the stuffing and secure with small skewers. Spoon the remaining stuffing into the larger cavity, packing it loosely. Place any leftover stuffing in a baking dish, cover tightly, and set aside for placing in the oven when the turkey is done. Cross the drumsticks and, using kitchen string, tie the legs together. Tuck the wings underneath the body. Spread the surface of the turkey with 2 tablespoons of the butter; melt the remaining 2 tablespoons and set aside. Cover the pan with heavy-duty aluminum foil or with its lid.

❋ Roast, basting every 20 minutes with the pan juices and the melted butter, for 2½ hours. Uncover and continue to roast, basting often, until well browned, the juices run clear when a thigh is pierced with a knife, and an instant-read thermometer inserted into the thickest part of a thigh away from the bone registers 170°F (77°C), 1–1½ hours longer.

❋ Remove from the oven and let stand for 30 minutes. Meanwhile, bake the leftover stuffing for 30 minutes. Remove the skewers and string, spoon the stuffing into a bowl, carve the turkey, and arrange on a platter. Pass the stuffing at the table.

NUTRITIONAL ANALYSIS PER SERVING: Calories 727 (Kilojoules 3,053); Protein 58 g; Carbohydrates 63 g; Total Fat 28 g; Saturated Fat 11 g; Cholesterol 165 mg; Sodium 775 mg; Dietary Fiber 11 g

Venison Loin with Mushroom Sauce

SERVES 8

PREP TIME: 30 MINUTES, PLUS 12 HOURS FOR MARINATING

COOKING TIME: 40 MINUTES, PLUS 20 MINUTES FOR REHYDRATING MUSHROOMS

INGREDIENTS

1 boneless venison loin, 2–3 lb (1–1.5 kg)

½ cup (4 fl oz/125 ml) dry red wine

½ cup (2 oz/60 g) chopped shallots

6 juniper berries or 1½ tablespoons gin

1 teaspoon coarsely ground pepper

FOR THE MUSHROOM SAUCE

2 cups (16 fl oz/500 ml) beef broth

½ cup (about 1 oz/30 g) dried porcini mushrooms

¼ cup (2 oz/60 g) unsalted butter

¾ lb (375 g) assorted fresh mushrooms such as shiitake, morel, chanterelle, white button, and cremini, in any combination, brushed clean and sliced

1 small clove garlic, finely chopped

1 teaspoon fresh thyme leaves

½ teaspoon snipped fresh rosemary

salt and ground pepper to taste

COOKING TIP: Time the cooking of the venison carefully. Because the meat is so lean, it will toughen if overcooked; serve medium-rare.

❋ Place the venison in a shallow baking dish. Add the wine, shallots, juniper berries or gin, and pepper. Turn to coat the meat on all sides. Cover and refrigerate for at least 12 hours, or for up to 24 hours.

❋ The next day, make the mushroom sauce: In a saucepan over high heat, combine the beef broth and dried porcini. Bring to a boil, cover, reduce the heat to low, and simmer for 5 minutes. Remove from the heat and let stand for 20 minutes. Pour the mushrooms and broth through a fine-mesh sieve lined with dampened cheesecloth (muslin) placed over a bowl; reserve the liquid. If the porcini feel gritty, rinse with cold water. Squeeze dry and chop coarsely.

❋ In a frying pan over medium-low heat, melt the butter. Add the fresh mushrooms and sauté until tender, about 10 minutes. Stir in the reserved porcini, garlic, thyme, rosemary, salt, and pepper. Cook, stirring, until heated through, 1–2 minutes. Set aside in the pan.

❋ Preheat an oven to 400°F (200°C). Lift the venison from the marinade, reserving the marinade. Pat dry with paper towels. Heat a large, heavy nonstick frying pan over medium heat until a drop of water evaporates on contact. Add the venison and brown on all sides, about 6 minutes total. Transfer to a roasting pan and roast to desired doneness, 10–12 minutes for medium-rare. Transfer to a cutting board and cover with aluminum foil. Let rest while finishing the sauce.

❋ Place the roasting pan over medium-high heat. Add the reserved marinade, bring to a boil, and deglaze the pan, stirring to dislodge any browned bits from the pan bottom. Boil until reduced to ½ cup (4 fl oz/125 ml), about 5 minutes. Add the porcini liquid and boil until the combined liquids are reduced to 1 cup (8 fl oz/250 ml), about 5 minutes. Strain through a fine-mesh sieve into the pan holding the sautéed mushrooms. Reheat and season with salt and pepper.

❋ To serve, cut the venison across the grain into thin slices. Arrange the slices, slightly overlapping, on a warmed platter. Using a slotted spoon, lift out the mushrooms and arrange on top of the meat. Pass the remaining sauce at the table.

NUTRITIONAL ANALYSIS PER SERVING: Calories 255 (Kilojoules 1,071); Protein 35 g; Carbohydrates 6 g; Total Fat 9 g; Saturated Fat 5 g; Cholesterol 134 mg; Sodium 266 mg; Dietary Fiber 2 g

Winter White Lasagne

PREP TIME: 35 MINUTES

COOKING TIME: 1½ HOURS

INGREDIENTS

1 butternut squash, 1½ lb (750 g),
    halved lengthwise and seeds and
    fibers removed

12 dried lasagne noodles

6 tablespoons (3 oz/90 g) unsalted
    butter

6 tablespoons (2 oz/60 g) all-purpose
    (plain) flour

3 cups (24 fl oz/750 ml) half-and-half
    (half cream), heated

½ cup (2 oz/60 g) grated Parmesan
    cheese

¼ teaspoon grated nutmeg

salt and ground pepper to taste

2 cups (1 lb/500 g) ricotta cheese

½ cup (2 oz/60 g) grated pecorino
    romano cheese

2 eggs

¾ cup (1 oz/30 g) finely chopped
    fresh flat-leaf (Italian) parsley

pinch of ground cloves

2 tablespoons olive oil

14 oz (440 g) fresh mushrooms,
    brushed clean and thinly sliced

2 cloves garlic, finely chopped

1 cup (5 oz/155 g) crumbled
    Gorgonzola cheese

2 cups (8 oz/250 g) shredded
    fontina cheese

This meatless lasagne features five different cheeses. Feel free to make substitutions depending upon availability.

SERVES 8–10

❋ Preheat an oven to 350°F (180°C). Place the squash halves, cut sides down, in a baking pan and add a couple spoonfuls of water to the pan. Cover and bake until tender, about 35 minutes. Let cool, then peel and cut crosswise into thin slices. Set aside.

❋ Meanwhile, bring a large pot three-fourths full of salted water to a boil over high heat. Add the noodles, stir well, and cook until almost al dente, about 10 minutes or according to the package directions. Drain and immerse in cold water until ready to use.

❋ To make a Parmesan béchamel sauce, in a saucepan over low heat, melt the butter. Add the flour and cook, stirring, for 2 minutes. Gradually stir in the hot half-and-half and bring to a boil over low heat. Boil gently, stirring constantly, until thickened, about 5 minutes. Stir in the Parmesan cheese, nutmeg, salt, and pepper. Set aside. In a bowl, whisk together the ricotta and romano cheeses, eggs, ½ cup (⅔ oz/20 g) of the parsley, cloves, and pepper to taste. Set aside.

❋ In a frying pan over medium-high heat, warm the olive oil. Add the mushrooms and cook, stirring, until lightly browned, about 10 minutes. Add the remaining ¼ cup (⅓ oz/10 g) parsley, garlic, and salt and pepper to taste. Cook, stirring, for 2 minutes. Remove from the heat and set aside.

❋ If the oven has been turned off, reheat it to 350°F (180°C). Lightly butter a shallow 10-by-14-inch (25-by-35-cm) baking dish.

❋ Drain the noodles and pat dry with paper towels. Arrange 4 noodles, slightly overlapping, on the bottom of the prepared dish. Spread with the ricotta mixture and top with a layer of the squash slices. Add a second layer of noodles. Top with a layer of the mushrooms. Sprinkle with the Gorgonzola cheese. Top with a final layer of noodles. Pour the béchamel sauce over the top. Sprinkle evenly with the fontina cheese.

❋ Bake until the top is browned and bubbly, 45–55 minutes. Remove from the oven and let stand for 15 minutes. Cut into squares to serve.

NUTRITIONAL ANALYSIS PER SERVING: Calories 701 (Kilojoules 2,944); Protein 30 g; Carbohydrates 46 g; Total Fat 45 g; Saturated Fat 26 g; Cholesterol 178 mg; Sodium 1,006 mg; Dietary Fiber 3 g

Roast Duck with Cranberry Glaze and Cranberry Relish

PREP TIME: 15 MINUTES

COOKING TIME: 2½ HOURS

INGREDIENTS

2 ducks, 4½–5½ lb (2.25–2.75 kg)
  each, thawed in the refrigerator
  if frozen

2 tablespoons lemon juice

salt and ground pepper to taste

1 yellow onion, quartered

4 whole cloves

1 orange, quartered

2 bay leaves, plus extra for garnish
  (optional)

FOR THE GLAZE

1 can (1 lb/500 g) jellied cranberry
  sauce

2 tablespoons lemon juice

1 teaspoon grated lemon zest

½ teaspoon salt

¼ teaspoon ground cloves

FOR THE CRANBERRY RELISH

1 cup (8 oz/250 g) sugar

½ cup (4 fl oz/125 ml) water

3 cups (12 oz/375 g) fresh or frozen
  cranberries, plus fresh cranberries
  for garnish (optional)

½ cup (3 oz/90 g) golden raisins
  (sultanas)

2 teaspoons grated or finely
  chopped lemon zest

1 tablespoon aged red wine vinegar
  or fruit-flavored vinegar

ground pepper to taste

❋ Rinse the ducks and pat dry. Sprinkle inside and out with the lemon juice, salt, and pepper. Pierce each onion quarter with 1 whole clove. Stuff each duck cavity with 2 onion quarters, 2 orange quarters, and 1 bay leaf. Cross the drumsticks and, using kitchen string, tie the legs together. Using a knife tip, pierce the skin of each duck at 1-inch (2.5-cm) intervals to allow the fat to cook out from under the skin.

❋ Preheat an oven to 350°F (180°C).

❋ To make the glaze, in a saucepan over medium heat, combine the cranberry sauce, lemon juice, lemon zest, salt, and ground cloves. Heat, stirring, until melted, about 5 minutes. Lightly brush the entire surface of the ducks with some of the glaze. Arrange the ducks, breast sides up, on a rack in a large roasting pan.

❋ Roast, basting every 30 minutes with the cranberry glaze. As excess fat accumulates in the roasting pan, use a bulb baster to remove it. After the first hour of roasting, carefully turn over the ducks onto their breasts and roast, breasts down, for 1 hour. Then turn the ducks breasts up again and continue to roast until the breast skin is golden and crisp and the meat at the leg joint is cooked through when cut into with a sharp knife, about 30 minutes longer. The ducks should cook in about 2½ hours total.

❋ While the ducks are roasting, make the cranberry relish: In a large sauté pan, combine the sugar and water over medium-low heat. Cook, stirring, until the mixture turns a golden amber, 5–10 minutes. Add the cranberries, raisins, and lemon zest all at once. Cook, stirring to break up any sugar lumps, until the cranberries pop and the mixture is thick, about 10 minutes. Remove from the heat. Stir in the vinegar and pepper. Transfer to a bowl and serve warm or at room temperature.

❋ When the ducks are ready, transfer them to a cutting board and let stand for 10 minutes. Cut into quarters and arrange on a warmed platter. Garnish with fresh cranberries and bay leaves, if desired. Pass the relish at the table.

NUTRITIONAL ANALYSIS PER SERVING: Calories 835 (Kilojoules 3,507); Protein 37 g; Carbohydrates 49 g; Total Fat 54 g; Saturated Fat 19 g; Cholesterol 161 mg; Sodium 184 mg; Dietary Fiber 2 g

Maple-Glazed Salmon Fillet with Oven-Roasted Sweet Potatoes

PREP TIME: 15 MINUTES

COOKING TIME: 40 MINUTES

INGREDIENTS

4 orange-fleshed sweet potatoes, about 2 lb (1 kg) total weight, peeled and thinly sliced on the diagonal

2 tablespoons unsalted butter, melted

½ teaspoon salt, plus salt to taste

ground pepper to taste

pinch of ground cinnamon

⅓ cup (3 fl oz/80 ml) pure maple syrup

2 tablespoons Worcestershire sauce

1 whole skinless salmon fillet, about 1⅔ lb (815 g)

COOKING TIP: Heating the syrup to boiling thickens it just enough to coat the salmon and cook to a glaze.

A whole salmon fillet basted with maple syrup quickly cooks to perfection in this simple but elegant recipe. The maple syrup begins to give a caramelized edge to the potatoes just as the salmon is done. If you like, garnish with snipped fresh chives.

SERVES 6

❋ Preheat an oven to 400°F (200°C).

❋ In a bowl, toss the potatoes with the melted butter, ½ teaspoon salt, pepper, and cinnamon to coat evenly. Arrange in a single layer on a large baking sheet. Place in the oven and roast until the potatoes begin to brown on the bottom, about 20 minutes.

❋ Meanwhile, in a small saucepan, stir together the maple syrup and Worcestershire sauce. Place over medium heat and bring to a boil. Reduce the heat to low and cook until thickened and reduced by one-half, about 5 minutes. Remove from the heat and set aside.

❋ Run your fingers over the salmon fillet to detect any errant bones; remove and discard any you find. Sprinkle the salmon fillet with salt and pepper.

❋ Remove the baking sheet from the oven. Raise the oven temperature to 450°F (230°C). Carefully turn over the sweet potatoes and place the salmon fillet on top of them. Brush half of the maple mixture evenly on the salmon fillet. Return the baking sheet to the oven and roast for 10 minutes. Remove from the oven and baste the salmon with the remaining maple mixture. Return to the oven once again and roast until the flesh is opaque at the center when cut into with the tip of a knife at the thickest point, 5–10 minutes longer.

❋ To serve, divide the salmon into serving portions and arrange on warmed individual plates with the sweet potatoes.

NUTRITIONAL ANALYSIS PER SERVING: Calories 378 (Kilojoules 1,588); Protein 27 g; Carbohydrates 39 g; Total Fat 12 g; Saturated Fat 4 g; Cholesterol 80 mg; Sodium 320 mg; Dietary Fiber 3 g

Baked Ham with Orange-Mustard-Pepper Glaze

PREP TIME: 15 MINUTES

COOKING TIME: 1½ HOURS

INGREDIENTS

½ fully cooked bone-in or boneless
  butt end ham, about 6 lb (3 kg)

FOR THE GLAZE

¾ cup (7½ oz/235 g) orange
  marmalade

I tablespoon Dijon mustard

I tablespoon soy sauce

½ teaspoon coarsely ground pepper

A baked ham makes an impressive centerpiece on the dining
or buffet table.

SERVES 8

❀ Let the ham stand at room temperature for about 1 hour before
baking. Preheat an oven to 325°F (165°C).

❀ Unwrap the ham and wipe the surface with a damp paper towel.
Trim off any extra-thick layers of fat. Score the outside surface of the
ham in a diamond pattern, making crosscuts ½ inch (12 mm) apart.

❀ Place the ham in a large roasting pan, rounded side up. Bake for
30 minutes.

❀ Meanwhile, make the glaze: In a small bowl, stir together the
orange marmalade, mustard, soy sauce, and pepper.

❀ Remove the ham from the oven and spread half of the glaze over
the surface of the ham. Return to the oven and bake, basting every
20 minutes with the remaining glaze until it is used up. The ham will
take about 12–15 minutes per pound (500 g) and is done when an instant-
read thermometer inserted into the thickest part registers 140°F (60°C),
about 1 hour longer.

❀ Remove from the oven and transfer the ham to a warmed platter.
Cover loosely with aluminum foil. Let stand for 20 minutes before
carving. Slice and arrange on the platter to serve.

NUTRITIONAL ANALYSIS PER SERVING: Calories 282 (Kilojoules 1,184); Protein 36 g;
Carbohydrates 12 g; Total Fat 10 g; Saturated Fat 3 g; Cholesterol 90 mg; Sodium 2,118 mg;
Dietary Fiber 0 g

Glazed Turkey Breast with Corn Bread Stuffing

PREP TIME: 40 MINUTES

COOKING TIME: 2¼ HOURS

INGREDIENTS

FOR THE CORN BREAD STUFFING

I cup (5 oz/155 g) each all-purpose (plain) flour and yellow cornmeal

I tablespoon sugar

I tablespoon baking powder

1½ teaspoons salt

¼ teaspoon ground pepper, plus pepper to taste

I cup (8 fl oz/250 ml) milk

¼ cup (2 oz/60 g) unsalted butter, melted and cooled, plus ¼ cup (2 oz/60 g) unsalted butter

I egg

2 cups (8 oz/250 g) chopped sweet onion such as Vidalia

1½ cups (6 oz/185 g) peeled, cored, and chopped apple

I cup (4½ oz/140 g) each chopped celery and chopped pecans

I cinnamon stick

I bone-in turkey breast, 6–7 lb (3–3.5 kg), rinsed and patted dry

2 tablespoons lemon juice

salt and ground pepper to taste

2 tablespoons unsalted butter

⅓ cup (4 oz/125 g) honey

2 tablespoons lemon juice

I teaspoon ground cinnamon

¼ teaspoon ground allspice

fresh sage leaves (optional)

❋ To make the corn bread, preheat an oven to 400°F (200°C). Lightly butter a 9-inch (23-cm) square baking pan. In a bowl, combine the flour, cornmeal, sugar, baking powder, ½ teaspoon of the salt, and the ¼ teaspoon pepper. In a separate bowl, whisk together the milk, melted butter, and egg. Add to the cornmeal mixture and stir just until blended. The mixture will be lumpy. Transfer to the prepared pan, spreading evenly. Bake until the edges begin to pull away from the sides and the top is firm, about 20 minutes. Let cool completely, cut into squares, and then coarsely crumble into a large bowl.

❋ To make the stuffing, in a large frying pan over medium heat, melt the ¼ cup (2 oz/60 g) butter. Add the onion, apple, and celery. Sauté until softened, about 5 minutes. Add the pecans and sauté until golden, about 5 minutes. Add the corn bread crumbs, cinnamon stick, the remaining 1 teaspoon salt, and pepper to taste. Let cool slightly.

❋ Preheat the oven to 350°F (180°C). Place the turkey breast, skin side up, in an aluminum foil–lined roasting pan. Sprinkle inside and out with the lemon juice, salt, and pepper. Using your fingers, make a pocket on either side of the breastbone between the skin and the meat and spread the butter inside. Spoon about 1 cup (8 oz/250 g) stuffing into the neck opening. Secure the skin over the opening with a small skewer. Spoon the remaining stuffing into the large cavity, using the foil liner to hold it in place. Cover the breast loosely with more foil.

❋ Roast for 45 minutes. Meanwhile, make a glaze: In a small saucepan over low heat, combine the honey, lemon juice, cinnamon, and allspice. Bring to a boil, stirring to blend, then remove from the heat.

❋ Remove the breast from the oven, uncover, and coat with half of the glaze. Continue to roast uncovered, brushing with the remaining glaze every 15 minutes, for about 1 hour. It is done when an instant-read thermometer inserted into the thickest part away from the bone registers 160°F (71°C), or the juices run clear when it is pierced with a knife. Remove from the oven and let stand for 10 minutes in the pan. Spoon the stuffing into a serving bowl. Thinly slice the breast. Arrange on a warmed platter. Garnish with sage, if desired. Pass the stuffing.

NUTRITIONAL ANALYSIS PER SERVING: Calories 658 (Kilojoules 2,764); Protein 58 g; Carbohydrates 33 g; Total Fat 32 g; Saturated Fat 11 g; Cholesterol 185 mg; Sodium 492 mg; Dietary Fiber 2 g

Curried Cornish Hens with Spiced Confetti Couscous

PREP TIME: 30 MINUTES

COOKING TIME: 1 HOUR

INGREDIENTS

FOR THE CURRIED CORNISH HENS

4 teaspoons Madras curry powder

½ cup (4 oz/125 g) unsalted butter, at room temperature

1 teaspoon grated orange zest

salt and ground pepper to taste

8 Cornish hens, 1 lb (500 g) each

8 each: yellow onion wedges; whole cloves; peeled fresh ginger slices; orange zest strips (about 2 inches/ 5 cm long); garlic cloves, lightly crushed; and bay leaves

FOR THE COUSCOUS

4 cups (32 fl oz/1 l) chicken broth

1 cinnamon stick

1 orange zest strip, 2 inches (5 cm) long and ½ inch (12 mm) wide

1 slice peeled fresh ginger

salt to taste

2 cups (12 oz/375 g) couscous

¼ cup (2 oz/60 g) unsalted butter

1 cup (4 oz/125 g) chopped sweet onion such as Vidalia

1 cup (5 oz/155 g) peeled and diced carrot

1 cup (5 oz/155 g) English peas

½ cup (3 oz/90 g) dried currants

1 clove garlic, finely chopped

½ cup (2 oz/60 g) sliced (flaked) almonds, toasted

Curry powder is a complex mixture of spices. Toasting it in a hot, dry frying pan helps to enhance the individual flavors.

SERVES 8

❋ To make the curried Cornish hens, in a small, dry frying pan over low heat, toast the curry powder, shaking the pan, just until it begins to warm and give off its aroma, about 20 seconds. Remove from the heat and transfer to a small bowl. Add the butter, orange zest, and salt and pepper. Using a fork, mash the spices into the butter until well blended. Cover and refrigerate until the butter is hard, about 30 minutes.

❋ Meanwhile, preheat an oven to 350°F (180°C). Rinse the hens and pat dry. Sprinkle inside and outside with salt and pepper. Stick each onion wedge with a whole clove. Place 1 onion wedge, 1 ginger slice, 1 orange zest strip, 1 garlic clove, and 1 bay leaf in the cavity of each hen. Cross the drumsticks on each bird and, using kitchen string, tie together. Starting at the neck opening, loosen the breast skin from the meat to make a small pocket. Cut the curried butter into 8 pieces and slip 1 piece under the skin of each hen, positioning it in the center of each breast. Arrange the hens, breast sides up, in a large baking pan.

❋ Roast, basting with the pan juices every 20 minutes, until the hens are golden brown and the juices run clear when a thigh is pierced with a knife, about 1 hour.

❋ Meanwhile, prepare the couscous: In a wide saucepan over high heat, combine the broth, cinnamon stick, orange zest, ginger, and salt. Bring to a boil, cover, reduce the heat to very low, and cook until the broth is infused with the seasonings, about 10 minutes. Remove from the heat, stir in the couscous, cover, and let stand for 20 minutes.

❋ In a sauté pan over medium heat, melt the butter. Add the onion and carrot and sauté until the onion is golden, about 5 minutes. Stir in the peas, currants, and garlic and cook, stirring, until heated through, about 5 minutes. Remove from the heat; keep warm. When the couscous is ready, toss in the sautéed vegetables and almonds.

❋ Spoon the couscous onto a warmed platter. Remove the strings from the hens and arrange on top. Serve immediately.

NUTRITIONAL ANALYSIS PER SERVING: Calories 947 (Kilojoules 3,977); Protein 53 g; Carbohydrates 53 g; Total Fat 57 g; Saturated Fat 21 g; Cholesterol 296 mg; Sodium 808 mg; Dietary Fiber 5 g

Beef Brisket with Caramelized Onions and Merlot Sauce

PREP TIME: 45 MINUTES

COOKING TIME: 3½ HOURS,
  PLUS 2 HOURS FOR
  CHILLING

INGREDIENTS

salt and ground pepper to taste

1 first or flat cut brisket, 4–5 lb
  (2–2.5 kg)

2 tablespoons olive oil

1½ cups (6 oz/185 g) chopped
  yellow onion

½ cup (2½ oz/75 g) diced carrot

2 cloves garlic, finely chopped

1 can (28 oz/875 g) plum (Roma)
  tomatoes, with juices

2 cups (16 fl oz/500 ml) Merlot or
  other full-bodied red wine

1 bay leaf

FOR THE CARAMELIZED ONIONS
2 tablespoons olive oil

3 cups (10½ oz/330 g) thinly sliced
  sweet onions such as Vidalia

salt and ground pepper to taste

½ cup (2 oz/60 g) pitted dried
  cherries

SERVING TIP: Before cutting the
brisket, look carefully at the grain,
which runs in long "strings" in one
direction. For the best texture, make
sure to cut across the grain.

For the best flavor, prepare this brisket a day before serving so
it can be cut into thin slices when cold and then reheated.

SERVES 8

❋ Preheat an oven to 325°F (165°C). Salt and pepper the brisket on
all sides. In a dutch oven or a large, wide ovenproof pan with a tight-
fitting lid, warm the olive oil over medium-high heat. Add the brisket
and brown well on both sides, about 6 minutes total. Transfer to a plate.
Add the onion and carrot to the pan and sauté until golden, about
5 minutes. Add the garlic and sauté until softened, about 1 minute.
Add the tomatoes and juices, 1 cup (8 fl oz/250 ml) of the wine, and
the bay leaf. Mix well and bring to a boil. Return the brisket to the pan,
cover, and place in the oven.

❋ Cook, basting occasionally with the pan juices, until fork tender,
about 3 hours. Remove from the oven and let cool in the juices.
Carefully lift the brisket from the juices and transfer it to a deep platter.
Cover with aluminum foil and refrigerate until cold, at least 2 hours or
up to overnight. Let the pan juices cool, then pass through a food mill
or press through a sieve into a bowl and set aside. Discard the solids.

❋ Just before serving, preheat the oven to 350°F (180°C). Cut the
brisket across the grain into thin slices. Arrange the slices, slightly
overlapping, on an ovenproof serving platter. Cover with aluminum
foil and place in the oven for 15 minutes to heat through.

❋ Meanwhile, cook the onions: In a large frying pan over medium-low
heat, warm the olive oil. Add the onions and sauté, stirring often, until
golden brown, about 20 minutes. Season with salt and pepper. While
the onions are cooking, pour the remaining 1 cup (8 fl oz/250 ml) wine
into a saucepan. Add ¼ cup (1 oz/30 g) of the dried cherries and bring
to a boil over high heat. Boil until reduced by one-half, about 5 minutes. Stir in the puréed brisket juices and return to a boil. Season to
taste with salt and pepper.

❋ To serve, remove the brisket from the oven. Pour the sauce evenly
over the top. Top with the caramelized onions and the remaining
¼ cup (1 oz/30 g) dried cherries. Serve immediately.

NUTRITIONAL ANALYSIS PER SERVING: Calories 871 (Kilojoules 3,658); Protein 48 g;
Carbohydrates 17 g; Total Fat 68 g; Saturated Fat 25 g; Cholesterol 179 mg; Sodium 331 mg;
Dietary Fiber 2 g

Roasted Carrots, Parsnips, and Garlic with Thyme

PREP TIME: 15 MINUTES

COOKING TIME: 55 MINUTES

INGREDIENTS

1 lb (500 g) parsnips, peeled and
  cut on the diagonal into slices
  ½-inch (12-mm) thick

1 lb (500 g) carrots, peeled and
  cut on the diagonal into slices
  ½-inch (12-mm) thick

12 cloves garlic, peeled but left whole

1 tablespoon fresh thyme leaves or
  1 teaspoon dried thyme, plus
  fresh sprigs for garnish (optional)

salt and ground pepper to taste

¼ cup (2 oz/60 g) unsalted butter,
  cut into small pieces

Add a splash of color to any holiday meal with carrots and parsnips, a perfect partnership of flavor and texture. In this oven-roasted dish, the root vegetables cook along with whole garlic cloves until caramelized and soft. Thyme makes an ideal herbal accent.

SERVES 6–8

❁ Preheat an oven to 350°F (180°C).

❁ In a 10-inch (25-cm) pie dish or baking dish, combine the parsnips, carrots, and garlic. If using fresh thyme, add half at this time. If using dried thyme, add it all, then season with salt and pepper. Toss to blend. Dot with the butter.

❁ Bake, stirring occasionally, until the vegetables are tender and lightly browned, about 55 minutes. Season with salt and pepper and add the remaining fresh thyme leaves, if using. Transfer to a serving dish and garnish with thyme sprigs, if using. Serve warm.

NUTRITIONAL ANALYSIS PER SERVING: Calories 132 (Kilojoules 554); Protein 2 g; Carbohydrates 18 g; Total Fat 7 g; Saturated Fat 4 g; Cholesterol 18 mg; Sodium 28 mg; Dietary Fiber 4 g

Sweet and White Potato Gratin

PREP TIME: 30 MINUTES

COOKING TIME: 1½ HOURS

INGREDIENTS

1½ lb (750 g) russet potatoes, peeled and thinly sliced

1 lb (500 g) sweet potatoes, peeled and thinly sliced

1½ cups (6 oz/185 g) coarsely shredded fontina cheese

¼ lb (125 g) fresh goat cheese, crumbled

¼ cup (1 oz/30 g) grated Parmesan cheese

2 teaspoons fresh thyme leaves

1 teaspoon salt

ground pepper to taste

2 tablespoons all-purpose (plain) flour

1 cup (8 fl oz/250 ml) heavy (double) cream

1 cup (8 fl oz/250 ml) chicken broth

¼ cup (2 oz/60 g) unsalted butter

2 cups (4 oz/125 g) fresh bread crumbs made from 4 slices firm white bread with crusts removed

PREP TIP: To keep peeled potatoes from turning brown, add them to a bowl of cold water. Drain well and pat dry with paper towels before using.

In this contemporary version of scalloped potatoes, the orange-fleshed sweet potatoes and white-fleshed russet potatoes combine to make an interesting contrast, visually and texturally. This is the perfect dish for a large gathering. It serves 8 generously and is elegant enough to serve directly from the baking dish at the table or for a buffet.

SERVES 8

❀ Preheat an oven to 350°F (180°C). Lightly butter a 9-by-13-by-2-inch (23-by-33-by-5-cm) baking dish.

❀ Using half of the potato and sweet potato slices, arrange them, slightly overlapping, in the prepared baking dish, alternating the white and sweet potatoes randomly.

❀ In a bowl, combine the fontina cheese, goat cheese, Parmesan cheese, thyme, salt, and pepper. Stir to blend. Sprinkle half of the cheese mixture over the potatoes. Sprinkle evenly with the flour. Arrange the remaining potato and sweet potato slices on top, again slightly overlapping and alternating randomly. Sprinkle evenly with the remaining cheese mixture. Pour the cream and broth over the potatoes. Cover loosely with aluminum foil.

❀ Bake until the potatoes are tender, about 1 hour.

❀ Meanwhile, in a sauté pan over low heat, melt the butter. Add the bread crumbs and toss to coat. Remove from the heat.

❀ Remove the potatoes from the oven and uncover. Sprinkle the buttered crumbs evenly over the surface. Return to the oven, uncovered, and bake until the top is crisped and brown, about 25 minutes longer. Remove from the oven and let stand at least 20 minutes before serving, then serve directly from the dish.

NUTRITIONAL ANALYSIS PER SERVING: Calories 448 (Kilojoules 1,882); Protein 14 g; Carbohydrates 32 g; Total Fat 30 g; Saturated Fat 18 g; Cholesterol 96 mg; Sodium 808 mg; Dietary Fiber 3 g

Haricots Verts with Toasted Almond Butter

PREP TIME: 20 MINUTES

COOKING TIME: 5 MINUTES

INGREDIENTS

1 cup (3½ oz/105 g) sliced (flaked) almonds

3 tablespoons cold unsalted butter, cut into pieces

2 teaspoons grated lemon zest

2 lb (1 kg) haricots verts or other slender green beans, stem ends trimmed

1 tablespoon kosher or coarse salt, plus salt to taste

freshly ground pepper to taste

PREP TIP: Trim only the stem ends of the haricots verts, leaving the delicate blossom ends intact.

Haricots verts are small, slender, very tender French green beans. The toasted almond butter adds a festive touch.

SERVES 6–8

❀ In a dry frying pan over medium-low heat, toast the almonds, stirring often, until golden brown, about 5 minutes. Remove from the heat and let cool.

❀ Transfer the almonds to a food processor and pulse to chop finely. With the motor running, add the butter pieces and lemon zest and process just until blended. Scrape into a small bowl and set aside.

❀ Bring a large pot three-fourths full of water to a boil over high heat. Stir in the beans and the 1 tablespoon salt. Cook, stirring occasionally, until the beans are tender but still bright green, 3–5 minutes; the timing will depend upon the size of the beans. Drain immediately.

❀ Transfer to a warmed serving bowl. Dot with the almond butter and toss to coat. Sprinkle with a little coarse salt and add a grinding of pepper. Serve immediately.

NUTRITIONAL ANALYSIS PER SERVING: Calories 163 (Kilojoules 685); Protein 5 g; Carbohydrates 11 g; Total Fat 12 g; Saturated Fat 4 g; Cholesterol 13 mg; Sodium 220 mg; Dietary Fiber 3 g

Parmesan Cornmeal Spoon Bread

PREP TIME: 20 MINUTES

COOKING TIME: 1 HOUR

INGREDIENTS

1 tablespoon unsalted butter

½ cup (2½ oz/75 g) finely
   chopped yellow onion

¼ cup (1½ oz/45 g) minced red
   bell pepper (capsicum)

1 clove garlic, crushed

1 cup (8 fl oz/250 ml) milk

1¾ cups (14 fl oz/430 ml) water

¾ cup (4 oz/125 g) yellow cornmeal

⅔ cup (2½ oz/75 g) grated Italian
   Parmesan cheese

¾ teaspoon salt, plus pinch of salt

⅛ teaspoon cayenne pepper

3 eggs, separated

SERVING TIP: The spoon bread can also be made in one 1-quart (1-l) soufflé dish. Baking time is 45 minutes. Alternatively, bake the batter in miniature (8-oz/250-g) pumpkins: First steam the pumpkins until tender, about 20 minutes. Let cool, then cut off the tops, scoop out the seeds and pulp, fill with the batter, and bake for 30 minutes.

Spoon bread is a cross between a firm soufflé and a soft quick bread. It puffs up when hot and deflates slightly as it cools. Serve hot as a side dish in place of potatoes.

SERVES 8

❀ Preheat an oven to 375°F (190°C). Lightly butter eight ½-cup (4–fl oz/ 125-ml) individual soufflé dishes.

❀ In a frying pan over medium-low heat, melt the butter. Add the onion and bell pepper and sauté until the onion is golden, about 5 minutes. Stir in the garlic and cook until softened, about 1 minute. Remove from the heat and set aside to cool.

❀ Pour the milk into a saucepan, place over medium heat, and bring just to a boil. Meanwhile, pour the water into a bowl and gradually stir in the cornmeal until smooth. When the milk has come to a boil, add the cornmeal mixture and cook, stirring, over medium heat, until thick, about 5 minutes. Stir in the Parmesan, ¼ teaspoon salt, and the cayenne pepper. Remove from the heat and let cool for about 15 minutes.

❀ Meanwhile, in a large bowl, whisk the egg yolks until blended. Gradually stir the cooled cornmeal mixture and the cooled onion mixture into the yolks until blended.

❀ In a separate bowl, combine the egg whites and a pinch of salt and whisk or beat with an electric mixer until soft peaks form. Using a rubber spatula, fold the egg whites into the cornmeal-onion mixture just until blended. Spoon into the prepared dishes, dividing it evenly.

❀ Bake until the tops are slightly puffed and browned, about 30 minutes. Serve immediately.

NUTRITIONAL ANALYSIS PER SERVING: Calories 155 (Kilojoules 651); Protein 8 g; Carbohydrates 14 g; Total Fat 7 g; Saturated Fat 4 g; Cholesterol 95 mg; Sodium 417 mg; Dietary Fiber 1 g

Braised Red Cabbage with Apple, Currants, and Aged Cider Vinegar

PREP TIME: 10 MINUTES

COOKING TIME: 18 MINUTES

INGREDIENTS

¼ cup (2 fl oz/60 ml) olive oil

1 head red cabbage, (about 2 lb/1 kg), cored and thinly sliced

1 Golden Delicious or other firm cooking apple, cored, peeled, and diced

¼ cup (1½ oz/45 g) dried currants or raisins

½ cup (4 fl oz/125 ml) aged cider vinegar, or to taste

2 tablespoons sugar

1 teaspoon salt, plus salt to taste

freshly ground pepper to taste

2 tablespoons fresh flat-leaf (Italian) parsley leaves (optional)

Sweet-and-sour cabbage with apples is traditionally served with pork or ham. For this holiday version, use red cabbage, which will cook to a brilliant fuchsia color. The dried currants, apple, and sugar all add a touch of sweetness, while the vinegar contributes a pleasantly sour bite.

SERVES 8

❀ In a large, deep sauté pan over medium heat, warm the olive oil. Add the cabbage, apple, and currants or raisins and stir to coat. Cover and cook until the cabbage is tender-crisp, about 10 minutes.

❀ Uncover and sprinkle with ¼ cup (2 fl oz/60 ml) of the vinegar, the sugar, and 1 teaspoon salt. Cook, stirring, until the cabbage is tender, about 8 minutes longer. Taste and adjust the seasonings with vinegar, salt, and a grinding of pepper.

❀ Remove from the heat and toss in the parsley, if using. Transfer to a warmed serving bowl and serve immediately.

NUTRITIONAL ANALYSIS PER SERVING: Calories 121 (Kilojoules 508); Protein 1 g; Carbohydrates 15 g; Total Fat 7 g; Saturated Fat 1 g; Cholesterol 0 mg; Sodium 302 mg; Dietary Fiber 2 g

Mixed Rice Pilaf with Dried Cherries, Apricots, and Cinnamon

PREP TIME: 20 MINUTES

COOKING TIME: 55 MINUTES

INGREDIENTS

2 tablespoons unsalted butter

1 cup (4 oz/125 g) chopped sweet onion such as Vidalia

2 teaspoons curry powder

1½ cups (10½ oz/330 g) brown basmati rice

½ cup (3 oz/90 g) wild rice

1 cinnamon stick

1 orange zest strip, 3 inches (7.5 cm) long and ½ inch (12 mm) wide, plus extra for garnish (optional)

4½ cups (36 fl oz/1.1 l) reduced-sodium chicken broth

½ cup (3 oz/90 g) dried apricots, cut into pieces

½ cup (2 oz/60 g) dried pitted cherries

½ cup (2 oz/60 g) sliced natural almonds

PREP TIP: Instead of mixing individual rices yourself, use one of the many mixed rice blends now available in food stores.

The trademark of a true pilaf is that the rice (or other grain) is always first sautéed in butter before the broth is added. This special-occasion pilaf, made nontraditionally with brown basmati and wild rices, arrives punctuated with dried apricots and cherries. You can substitute raisins for the cherries and omit the apricots, if you like.

SERVES 6–8

❁ In a large, wide saucepan over low heat, melt the butter. Add the onion and sauté, stirring, until golden, about 5 minutes. Add the curry powder and stir to blend. Stir in the brown basmati rice, wild rice, cinnamon stick, and orange zest. Cook, stirring, for 2 minutes.

❁ Add the broth, apricots, and cherries and raise the heat to high. Bring to a boil, stirring once. Cover, reduce the heat to medium-low, and cook until the broth is absorbed and the rice is tender, about 55 minutes. Remove from the heat and let stand, covered, for 10 minutes.

❁ Meanwhile, in a small, dry frying pan over medium-low heat, toast the almonds, stirring constantly, until golden, about 3 minutes. Remove from the heat.

❁ Spoon the pilaf into a warmed serving bowl, discarding the cinnamon stick and orange zest. Sprinkle with the toasted almonds and additional orange zest, if using. Serve immediately.

NUTRITIONAL ANALYSIS PER SERVING: Calories 365 (Kilojoules 1,533); Protein 10 g; Carbohydrates 60 g; Total Fat 10 g; Saturated Fat 3 g; Cholesterol 9 mg; Sodium 366 mg; Dietary Fiber 2 g

Pan-Roasted Shallots with Sherry Wine Glaze

PREP TIME: 15 MINUTES

COOKING TIME: 45 MINUTES

INGREDIENTS

2 lb (1 kg) shallots, halved length-
    wise if large

2 tablespoons olive oil

2 teaspoons dried sage

½ teaspoon salt, plus salt to taste

freshly ground pepper to taste

¾ cup (6 fl oz/180 ml) sweet sherry

fresh sage leaves (optional)

PREP TIP: If shallots arc unavailable, small white onions can be used for this recipe. To peel the onions quickly, blanch them in boiling water for 5 minutes, drain, and rinse with cold water. The skins will peel right off.

Shallots, which are composed of multiple cloves much like a head of garlic, have a mild onion flavor. They are a delicious alternative to the old-fashioned pearl onions that are typically part of a holiday meal. Shallots are available in many sizes, but larger ones are easier to peel, cutting the preparation time of this dish to a minimum.

SERVES 4–6

❀ Preheat an oven to 400°F (200°C).

❀ In a 10-inch (25-cm) pie dish or baking dish, combine the shallots, olive oil, 1 teaspoon of the dried sage, ½ teaspoon salt, and a grinding of pepper. Toss to mix well. Roast, stirring once or twice, until the shallots are tender and golden, about 45 minutes.

❀ About 5 minutes before the shallots are done, pour the sherry into a small frying pan and bring to a boil over medium-high heat. Boil gently until reduced by one-half, about 5 minutes.

❀ Remove the dish from the oven, sprinkle the remaining 1 teaspoon dried sage over the sizzling shallots, and pour the reduced sherry on top. Season to taste with salt and pepper and toss to coat. Transfer to a serving dish. Garnish with fresh sage, if desired. Serve immediately.

NUTRITIONAL ANALYSIS PER SERVING: Calories 216 (Kilojoules 907); Protein 5 g; Carbohydrates 35 g; Total Fat 6 g; Saturated Fat 1 g; Cholesterol 0 mg; Sodium 257 mg; Dietary Fiber 1 g

Cranberry-Raspberry Granita

PREP TIME: 15 MINUTES,
    PLUS 4 HOURS FOR
    FREEZING

COOKING TIME: 10 MINUTES

INGREDIENTS

2½ cups (20 fl oz/625 ml) water

2 cups (8 oz/250 g) fresh or frozen cranberries

1 package (10 oz/315 g) frozen unsweetened raspberries, plus fresh or frozen raspberries for garnish (optional)

1½ cups (12 oz/375 g) sugar

MAKE-AHEAD TIP: Make this simple dessert up to 3 days before serving. Remember to let it stand at room temperature for at least 20 minutes, so it will have a chance to soften before you scoop it out.

Here, we combine a bit of summer, raspberries kept in the freezer, with the quintessential fall fruit, fresh cranberries. The natural sweetness of the raspberries and the astringent taste of the cranberries are delicious frozen together in this beautiful red sorbet.

MAKES 1 QT (1 L); SERVES 6–8

✳ In a saucepan, combine the water, cranberries, the package of raspberries, and the sugar. Bring to a boil over medium heat, reduce the heat to low, and cook, stirring, until the cranberries pop, about 5 minutes. Remove from the heat and let cool slightly. Pour the mixture through a large sieve placed over a bowl, pressing on the fruit with the back of a spoon to force as much pulp through as possible. Measure 1 cup (8 fl oz/250 ml) of the purée, cover, and refrigerate until ready to serve.

✳ Transfer the remaining purée to a shallow metal pan and place in a freezer. Freeze until the mixture is frozen around the edges but still slushy in the center, about 2 hours. Spoon into a food processor and purée until smooth. Pour back into the metal pan and refreeze until almost firm, about 1 hour. Purée again in the food processor. Then pack into a large plastic container with a tight-fitting lid and freeze until firm, at least 1 hour or for up to 3 days.

✳ Remove the granita from the freezer about 20 minutes before serving to soften slightly. Scoop into stemmed glasses and top each serving with 2 tablespoons of the reserved purée. Garnish with a few fresh or frozen whole raspberries, if using. Serve immediately.

NUTRITIONAL ANALYSIS PER SERVING: Calories 226 (Kilojoules 949); Protein 1 g; Carbohydrates 58 g; Total Fat 0 g; Saturated Fat 0 g; Cholesterol 0 mg; Sodium 1 mg; Dietary Fiber 1 g

Toasted Hazelnut Chocolate Custard

PREP TIME: 15 MINUTES, PLUS
1 HOUR FOR STEEPING

COOKING TIME: 15 MINUTES

INGREDIENTS

2 cups (10 oz/315 g) hazelnuts
  (filberts)

3 cups (24 fl oz/750 ml) heavy
  (double) cream

1 cup (8 fl oz/250 ml) milk

⅓ cup (3 oz/90 g) sugar

5 oz (155 g) bittersweet or semisweet (plain) chocolate, chopped,
  plus chocolate shaved into curls
  with a vegetable peeler for garnish

6 egg yolks

1 teaspoon vanilla extract (essence)

PREP TIP: To make chocolate curls,
it helps to slightly soften a block of
chocolate by warming it between
your hands. Then draw a vegetable
peeler along the surface.

For this decadent dessert, splurge on the best French or
Belgian bittersweet or semisweet chocolate available, such as
Valrhona or Callebaut.

SERVES 8

✳ Preheat an oven to 350°F (180°C). Spread the hazelnuts on a baking
sheet and toast until fragrant and the skins have loosened, 5–7 minutes.
While still warm, transfer to a kitchen towel and rub vigorously to
remove the skins. Do not worry if small bits remain. Reserve 8 whole
hazelnuts for garnish. Transfer the remaining nuts to a food processor
and process until very finely ground; do not overprocess.

✳ In a saucepan over medium heat, warm the cream and milk until
bubbles appear along the pan edges. Stir in the ground nuts, simmer
for 3 minutes, cover, and set aside to steep for 1 hour.

✳ Line a sieve with a double thickness of dampened cheesecloth (muslin) and place over a heatproof bowl. Pour the cream mixture through
the sieve, pressing on the solids with the back of a spoon to extract as
much hazelnut flavor as possible, then squeeze the cheesecloth with
your hands to extract any additional liquid. Add the sugar to the bowl
and stir well. Set over (not touching) very hot water in a saucepan over
medium heat. Add the 5 oz (155 g) chocolate and heat, stirring, until
the chocolate melts, about 5 minutes.

✳ In another bowl, whisk the egg yolks until blended. Add about ½ cup
(4 fl oz/125 ml) of the hot chocolate cream, whisking constantly. Then
whisk the yolks into the chocolate cream. Place the bowl over the hot
water in the saucepan and cook, stirring often, just until thick enough
to coat the back of a spoon, about 10 minutes. Remove from the heat,
stir in the vanilla, and pour through a fine-mesh sieve into a pitcher.
Then pour into eight ½-cup (4–fl oz/125-ml) ramekins. Let cool to room
temperature, or refrigerate until chilled.

✳ Garnish each custard with chocolate shavings and a whole hazelnut.
Serve at room temperature or chilled.

NUTRITIONAL ANALYSIS PER SERVING: Calories 545 (Kilojoules 2,289); Protein 7 g;
Carbohydrates 25 g; Total Fat 48 g; Saturated Fat 26 g; Cholesterol 286 mg; Sodium 54 mg;
Dietary Fiber 1 g

Caramelized Pear, Lemon, and Currant Tart

PREP TIME: 25 MINUTES,
    PLUS 1 HOUR FOR CHILLING

COOKING TIME: 40 MINUTES

INGREDIENTS

FOR THE PASTRY

1½ cups (7½ oz/235 g) all-purpose (plain) flour

1 tablespoon sugar

½ teaspoon salt

½ cup (4 oz/125 g) plus 2 tablespoons cold unsalted butter, cut into small pieces

4–5 tablespoons (2–2½ fl oz/ 60–75 ml) ice water

FOR THE FILLING

3 tablespoons unsalted butter

5 tablespoons (3 oz/90 g) sugar

5 firm but ripe Bosc pears, about 1¾ lb (875 g) total weight, peeled, quartered, and cored

1 tablespoon lemon juice

1 teaspoon grated or finely minced lemon zest, plus zest strips for garnish

pinch of grated nutmeg

2 tablespoons dried currants

whipped cream (optional)

This adaptation of the famous French upside-down tart known as a *tarte Tatin* uses pears in place of apples.

SERVES 6–8

❋ To make the pastry, in a food processor, combine the flour, sugar, and salt; process briefly to blend. Add the butter and pulse until the mixture forms pea-sized pieces. Transfer the mixture to a large bowl. Sprinkle with the ice water, 1 tablespoon at a time, tossing lightly with a fork until the dough comes together in a loose ball. Flatten into a disk and wrap in aluminum foil. Refrigerate for 1–2 hours.

❋ Position a rack in the lower third of an oven. Preheat to 400°F (200°C).

❋ To make the filling, combine 2 tablespoons of the butter and 4 tablespoons (2 oz/60 g) of the sugar in a heavy ovenproof frying pan about 10 inches (25 cm) in diameter and 2 inches (5 cm) deep. Place over medium heat and cook, stirring occasionally, until amber in color, about 5 minutes.

❋ In a bowl, toss together the pears, lemon juice, lemon zest, and nutmeg. Arrange the pears, rounded sides down, in a tight circle in the pan, filling in every space. Sprinkle with the currants. Place over medium-low heat and cook for 5 minutes, shaking the pan gently so the pears are coated with the caramelized sugar. Remove from the heat. Cut the remaining 1 tablespoon butter into bits, then dot the surface with it. Sprinkle with the remaining 1 tablespoon sugar.

❋ On a lightly floured work surface, roll out the dough into a round about 11 inches (28 cm) in diameter. Fold in the edges ½ inch (12 mm) to make a thick rim. Pierce all over with a fork. Transfer the pastry to the pan, covering the pear mixture completely and tucking the edges inside the pan.

❋ Bake until the pastry is golden and the juices are bubbling up the sides of pan, 35–40 minutes. Remove from the oven and let stand for 5 minutes. Invert a serving plate over the frying pan, then invert them together. Lift off the pan. Garnish with strips of lemon zest. Serve warm or at room temperature. Accompany with whipped cream, if desired.

NUTRITIONAL ANALYSIS PER SERVING: Calories 544 (Kilojoules 2,285); Protein 5 g; Carbohydrates 57 g; Total Fat 35 g; Saturated Fat 21 g; Cholesterol 104 mg; Sodium 183 mg; Dietary Fiber 4 g

Chocolate Roulade with Chocolate Brandy Sauce

SERVES 10–12

PREP TIME: 1 HOUR, PLUS
3 HOURS FOR CHILLING

COOKING TIME: 25 MINUTES

INGREDIENTS

FOR THE CAPPUCCINO CREAM
1½ cups (12 fl oz/375 ml) heavy
(double) cream

¼ cup (2 fl oz/60 ml) cold brewed
espresso

1 teaspoon vanilla extract (essence)

¼ cup (1 oz/30 g) sifted confectioners'
(icing) sugar

FOR THE CHOCOLATE SPONGE CAKE
8 eggs, separated, at room
temperature

pinch of salt

½ cup (4 oz/125 g) granulated sugar

1 teaspoon vanilla extract (essence)

½ cup (1½ oz/45 g) sifted cocoa,
preferably Dutch process

¼ cup (¾ oz/20 g) each sifted all-
purpose (plain) flour and sifted
cornstarch (cornflour)

confectioners' (icing) sugar

FOR THE CHOCOLATE BRANDY SAUCE
1½ cups (12 fl oz/375 ml) heavy
(double) cream

4 oz (125 g) semisweet (plain)
chocolate, chopped

2 tablespoons granulated sugar

2 tablespoons brandy

10 –12 strawberries (optional)

❀ To begin making the cappuccino cream, in a bowl, stir together the cream and espresso. Cover and chill well, about 3 hours.

❀ To make the chocolate sponge cake, preheat an oven to 400°F (200°C). Lightly butter an 11-by-16-inch (28-by-40-cm) jelly-roll (Swiss-roll) pan. Line the bottom with waxed paper or parchment (baking) paper. Lightly butter the paper and then dust with a little flour.

❀ In a large bowl, using an electric mixer, beat the egg whites with the salt until soft peaks form. Gradually beat in the granulated sugar, 1 tablespoon at a time. Beat until stiff peaks form, about 5 minutes. In a third bowl, beat together the egg yolks and vanilla. Fold one-fourth of the beaten whites into the yolks until blended. Spoon the egg yolk mixture onto the remaining whites, sprinkle the cocoa and flour mixture over the top, and fold together. Pour into the prepared pan, spreading evenly. Bake until set to the touch, about 12 minutes.

❀ Meanwhile, sprinkle a large kitchen towel with confectioners' sugar. When the cake is ready, remove from the oven and loosen the pan sides. Place the towel, sugar side down, on top and invert onto a work surface. Lift off the pan, peel off the paper, and let cool.

❀ To finish the cappuccino cream, pour the chilled cream-and-espresso mixture into a chilled bowl. Add the vanilla and beat until soft peaks form. Sprinkle with the confectioners' sugar and beat until stiff.

❀ Spread the cappuccino cream on the sponge to within 1 inch (2.5 cm) of the edges. Starting at one of the short sides, roll up the sponge and place on a platter, seam side down. Sift confectioners' sugar on top.

❀ To make the sauce, in a saucepan over medium heat, combine the cream, chocolate, and granulated sugar. Heat, stirring constantly, until the chocolate melts. Bring to a rolling boil and cook until thick, about 5 minutes. Remove from the heat and stir in the brandy.

❀ Slice the roulade and serve each slice on a pool of the sauce. Garnish with the strawberries, if desired.

NUTRITIONAL ANALYSIS PER SERVING: Calories 432 (Kilojoules 1,814); Protein 7 g; Carbohydrates 32 g; Total Fat 31 g; Saturated Fat 18 g; Cholesterol 243 mg; Sodium 113 mg; Dietary Fiber 0 g

Steamed Fig Pudding with Orange-Caramel Cream Sauce

PREP TIME: 40 MINUTES,
   PLUS 1 HOUR FOR SOAKING

COOKING TIME: 2 HOURS

INGREDIENTS

6 dried Mission or Calimyrna figs,
   hard stems trimmed, then halved
   through the stem ends, plus
   ½ cup (3 oz/90 g) minced dried figs

3 tablespoons Grand Marnier or
   other orange liqueur

¾ cup (4½ oz/140 g) raisins

1 tablespoon plus ½ cup (2½ oz/75 g)
   all-purpose (plain) flour

1 teaspoon grated orange zest

½ cup (4 oz/125 g) unsalted butter,
   at room temperature

½ cup (3½ oz/105 g) firmly packed
   light brown sugar

3 eggs, lightly beaten

1 teaspoon baking powder

¾ cup (1½ oz/45 g) fresh fine white
   bread crumbs

½ cup (4 fl oz/125 ml) orange juice

1 teaspoon vanilla extract (essence)

FOR THE SAUCE

½ cup (4 oz/125 g) granulated sugar

¼ cup (2 fl oz/60 ml) orange juice

1¼ cups (10 fl oz/310 ml) heavy
   (double) cream

½ teaspoon grated orange zest

1 teaspoon vanilla extract (essence)

Steamed puddings are classic holiday desserts in England. Although this pudding is cakelike, use a spoon for serving.

SERVES 6

✽ In a small bowl, combine the halved figs and the Grand Marnier or other liqueur. Cover and let stand for at least 1 hour or up to overnight.

✽ Butter a 1-qt (1-l) pudding mold with lid or a heatproof bowl. Arrange the fig halves, rounded sides down, on the bottom. Place a rack or a folded kitchen towel in the bottom of a deep pot. Pour in water to a depth of 3 inches (7.5 cm) and bring to a gentle simmer.

✽ Meanwhile, in a bowl, combine the minced figs, raisins, the 1 tablespoon flour, and the orange zest. Toss to combine. In a large bowl, beat together the butter and brown sugar until creamy. Add the eggs and beat just until blended. In another small bowl, stir together the ½ cup (2½ oz/75 g) flour and the baking powder. Stir into the butter mixture. Stir in the bread crumbs. Mix in the orange juice and vanilla. Fold in the fig-raisin mixture. Spoon into the prepared pudding mold or bowl. Cover with a piece of buttered waxed paper, buttered side down. Secure the lid on the mold, or cover the bowl with aluminum foil and secure with kitchen string. Place the container on the rack or towel and cover the pot. Steam the pudding until set, about 2 hours, adding simmering water to the pot as needed to maintain the original level.

✽ Meanwhile, make the sauce: In a heavy frying pan over medium heat, melt the granulated sugar until it turns dark amber. Add the orange juice all at once, then the cream. The sugar will harden and turn gummy immediately, but continue to cook, pushing gently at the sugar with a wooden spoon, until the cream boils and the sugar melts again, about 10 minutes. Bring to a rolling boil and remove from the heat. Stir in the orange zest and vanilla. Set aside.

✽ Remove the mold or bowl from the pot and let stand, covered, for 15 minutes. Uncover and unmold onto a serving plate. Serve warm or at room temperature. To serve, pour a pool of the sauce onto each individual plate and, using a large spoon, divide the pudding among the plates.

NUTRITIONAL ANALYSIS PER SERVING: Calories 731 (Kilojoules 3,070); Protein 8 g; Carbohydrates 95 g; Total Fat 38 g; Saturated Fat 22 g; Cholesterol 218 mg; Sodium 182 mg; Dietary Fiber 5 g

Ginger Sour Cream Cheesecake with Gingersnap Crust

PREP TIME: 25 MINUTES

COOKING TIME: 1¼ HOURS,
    PLUS 6 HOURS FOR
    CHILLING

INGREDIENTS

FOR THE CRUST

20 gingersnap cookies, finely crushed
    (about 1 cup/3 oz/90 g crumbs)

½ teaspoon ground cinnamon

2 tablespoons unsalted butter, melted

FOR THE FILLING

1½ lb (750 g) cream cheese, at
    room temperature

1 cup (8 oz/250 g) sugar

½ cup (1 oz/30 g) finely chopped
    crystallized ginger

3 eggs

2 cups (16 fl oz/500 ml) sour cream,
    stirred until smooth

PREP TIP: Gingersnaps are very hard
and crisp. To make crushing them
easier, first place them in a plastic
bag and break into small pieces with
a rolling pin or other blunt object.
Then transfer to a food processor to
finish the job.

This creamy cheesecake needs to chill for at least 6 hours, so plan your holiday cooking schedule with this in mind. The cake cooks to a rich golden color, with a morsel of crystallized ginger concealed in every mouthful.

SERVES 10–12

❀ Preheat an oven to 350°F (180°C). Lightly butter the bottom and sides of a 10-inch (25-cm) springform pan with 2½-inch (6-cm) sides.

❀ To make the crust, in a large bowl, combine the gingersnap crumbs and cinnamon; stir to blend. Drizzle with the melted butter and stir until evenly blended. Transfer to the prepared pan and press the crust in an even layer over the bottom and about ½ inch (12 mm) up the sides of the pan. Set aside until ready to fill.

❀ To make the filling, in a large bowl, using an electric mixer, beat the cream cheese until smooth. Gradually add the sugar and crystallized ginger and beat until blended. Beat in the eggs one at a time, beating well after each addition. Beat in the sour cream until blended. Pour the batter into the prepared pan.

❀ Bake until the top is lightly browned and the center is firm, about 1 hour and 10 minutes. Remove from the oven and place on a rack to cool slightly. Using a spatula, loosen the edges of the cheesecake from the sides of the pan; do not remove the pan sides. Cover the warm cheesecake with aluminum foil and place in the refrigerator until well chilled, at least 6 hours or up to overnight.

❀ To serve, uncover the cheesecake and release and lift off the pan sides. Slide the pan bottom onto a serving plate. Cut the cheesecake into thin wedges to serve.

NUTRITIONAL ANALYSIS PER SERVING: Calories 486 (Kilojoules 2,041); Protein 8 g; Carbohydrates 37 g; Total Fat 35 g; Saturated Fat 21 g; Cholesterol 151 mg; Sodium 278 mg; Dietary Fiber 0 g

Pumpkin Praline Pie

PREP TIME: 25 MINUTES, PLUS
1 HOUR FOR CHILLING

COOKING TIME: 50 MINUTES

INGREDIENTS

FOR THE PASTRY

1½ cups (7½ oz/235 g) all-purpose (plain) flour

1 tablespoon granulated sugar

½ teaspoon salt

¼ cup (2 oz/60 g) cold unsalted butter, cut into small pieces

¼ cup (2 oz/60 g) solid vegetable shortening

6–7 tablespoons (3–3½ fl oz/ 90–105 ml) ice water

1 egg white, lightly beaten

FOR THE FILLING

1 can (1 lb/500 g) pumpkin purée

½ cup (4 oz/125 g) granulated sugar

½ cup (3½ oz/105 g) firmly packed light brown sugar

½ teaspoon ground cinnamon

pinch of ground nutmeg

½ teaspoon salt

2 eggs

1 cup (8 fl oz/250 ml) heavy (double) cream

FOR THE PRALINE TOPPING

⅔ cup (5 oz/155 g) firmly packed light brown sugar

3 tablespoons unsalted butter, at room temperature

1 cup (4 oz/125 g) broken pecans

Pumpkin pie is the quintessential holiday dessert. In this festive rendition, the silky smooth pumpkin custard offers a perfect contrast to the crunch of the pecan praline topping.

SERVES 8

❋ To make the pastry, in a large bowl, stir together the flour, granulated sugar, and salt. Add the butter and shortening and, using a pastry blender or 2 knives, cut them into the flour mixture until it resembles coarse crumbs. Sprinkle with the ice water, 1 tablespoon at a time, tossing lightly with a fork until the mixture comes together in a loose ball. Flatten slightly and wrap in aluminum foil. Refrigerate for 1–2 hours.

❋ Preheat an oven to 425°F (220°C).

❋ On a lightly floured work surface, gently roll the dough out into a round 12 inches (30 cm) in diameter. Drape the round over the rolling pin and carefully transfer to a 9-inch (23-cm) pie pan, pressing it gently into the pan. Double-fold the edges under and crimp to make a rim about ½ inch (12 mm) high. Lightly brush the bottom of the pastry with the egg white. Set aside.

❋ To make the filling, in a large bowl, combine the pumpkin, granulated and brown sugars, cinnamon, nutmeg, salt, and eggs; whisk until blended. Gradually add the cream, stirring until blended. Pour into the prepared pie shell.

❋ Bake for 15 minutes. Reduce the oven temperature to 350°F (180°C) and bake for another 20 minutes.

❋ Meanwhile, make the praline topping: In a bowl, beat together the brown sugar and butter until blended. Stir in the pecans.

❋ Carefully pull out the oven rack with the partially baked pie and sprinkle the praline mixture evenly over the surface of the pie. Continue to bake until the filling is set and the praline topping is golden, about 15 minutes longer. Transfer to a rack and let cool completely before serving.

NUTRITIONAL ANALYSIS PER SERVING: Calories 664 (Kilojoules 2,789); Protein 7 g; Carbohydrates 74 g; Total Fat 39 g; Saturated Fat 16 g; Cholesterol 121 mg; Sodium 340 mg; Dietary Fiber 3 g

Caramelized Cashew Tartlets with Maple Whipped Cream

PREP TIME: 30 MINUTES

COOKING TIME: 35 MINUTES

INGREDIENTS

FOR THE PASTRY

1½ cups (7½ oz/235 g) all-purpose
   (plain) flour

3 tablespoons firmly packed light
   brown sugar

½ teaspoon salt

½ cup (4 oz/125 g) cold unsalted
   butter, cut into small pieces

1 egg yolk

1 teaspoon vanilla extract (essence)

FOR THE FILLING

½ cup (3½ oz/105 g) firmly packed
   light brown sugar

2 tablespoons all-purpose (plain) flour

¼ teaspoon salt

1 cup (10 oz/315 g) dark corn syrup

3 eggs

1 tablespoon unsalted butter, melted

1 teaspoon vanilla extract (essence)

3 cups (15 oz/470 g) unsalted
   cashews

FOR THE MAPLE WHIPPED CREAM

1 cup (8 fl oz/250 ml) chilled heavy
   (double) cream

¼ cup (2¾ fl oz/80 ml) maple syrup,
   chilled

The sweet, buttery flavor of cashew nuts makes these little tarts irresistible. They may also be served simply dusted with confectioners' (icing) sugar.

SERVES 8

❀ To make the pastry, in a food processor, combine the flour, brown sugar, and salt. Process until blended. Add the butter, a few pieces at a time, pulsing until the mixture is crumbly. In a small bowl, whisk together the egg yolk and vanilla. With the motor running, add the egg mixture to the flour mixture, processing just until the ingredients hold together in a dough. Turn out onto a lightly floured work surface.

❀ Have ready eight 3-inch (7.5-cm) tartlet pans with removable bottoms. Using floured hands, flatten the dough into a disk. Using a small, sharp knife, cut into 8 evenly sized wedges. Press each wedge evenly over the bottom and up the sides of the pans.

❀ Position a rack in the lower third of an oven. Preheat to 400°F (200°C).

❀ To make the filling, in a bowl, stir together the brown sugar, flour, and salt until blended. Add the corn syrup, eggs, butter, and vanilla. Whisk until thoroughly blended.

❀ Arrange the pastry-lined tartlet pans on a baking sheet. Spread an even layer of the cashews in each pastry shell. Pour the filling over the nuts, filling each shell about two-thirds full.

❀ Bake for 15 minutes. Reduce the oven temperature to 350°F (180°C) and bake until the filling is set and the pastry is browned, about 20 minutes longer. Transfer to a rack and let cool. When cool enough to handle, remove the pan sides and slide the tartlets off the pan bottoms onto racks to cool completely.

❀ Just before serving, make the whipped cream: In a bowl, combine the cream and maple syrup. Beat until soft peaks form.

❀ Place each tartlet on an individual plate with a spoonful of whipped cream alongside.

NUTRITIONAL ANALYSIS PER TARTLET: Calories 879 (Kilojoules 2,892); Protein 15 g; Carbohydrates 97 g; Total Fat 57 g; Saturated Fat 21 g; Cholesterol 182 mg; Sodium 234 mg; Dietary Fiber 3 g

Country-Style Brandied Apple and Dried Cherry Tart

PREP TIME: 30 MINUTES, PLUS
1 HOUR FOR CHILLING

COOKING TIME: 55 MINUTES

INGREDIENTS

FOR THE PASTRY

1½ cups (7½ oz/235 g) all-purpose
(plain) flour

1 tablespoon granulated sugar

½ teaspoon salt

½ cup (4 oz/125 g) cold unsalted
butter, cut into small pieces

6–7 tablespoons (3–3½ fl oz/
90–105 ml) ice water

FOR THE FILLING

¼ cup (1 oz/30 g) dried pitted cherries

2 tablespoons brandy

3 lb (1.5 kg) Golden Delicious or
other baking apples

¼ cup (2 oz/60 g) granulated sugar

2 tablespoons all-purpose (plain)
flour

confectioners' (icing) sugar

Graceful looking and easy to assemble, this free-form tart is baked on a baking sheet. It has an all-butter crust, although it can be made with half butter and half solid vegetable shortening, if preferred. If dried cherries are not available, substitute dried cranberries.

SERVES 8

❁ To make the pastry, in a large bowl, combine the flour, granulated sugar, and salt. Add the butter and, using a pastry blender or 2 knives, cut the butter into the flour mixture until it resembles coarse crumbs. Sprinkle with the ice water, 1 tablespoon at a time, tossing lightly with a fork until the dough comes together in a loose ball. Flatten into a disk and wrap in aluminum foil. Refrigerate for 1–2 hours.

❁ Meanwhile, make the filling: In a small bowl, combine the cherries and brandy. Cover and let stand until plump, about 30 minutes.

❁ Peel, quarter, and core the apples, then cut into ½-inch (12-mm) wedges. Place in a large bowl, add the cherries and brandy, and toss to coat. In a small bowl, stir together the granulated sugar and flour, then sprinkle over the apples.

❁ Position a rack in the lower third of an oven and preheat to 400°F (200°C). Lightly butter a large baking sheet.

❁ On a lightly floured work surface, roll out the dough into a round 13–14 inches (33–35 cm) in diameter. Carefully drape it over the rolling pin and transfer to the prepared baking sheet. Spread the apples on top of the crust, mounding them slightly in the center and leaving a 3–4-inch (7.5–10-cm) border uncovered. Fold up the crust edges to cover the apples partially, leaving the center uncovered.

❁ Bake for 15 minutes. Reduce the oven temperature to 350°F (180°C) and continue to bake until the crust is golden and the apple mixture is bubbly, about 40 minutes longer. Transfer to a rack and let cool completely. Carefully transfer to a serving platter or tray. Using a fine-mesh sieve, sift confectioners' sugar over the top. Cut into wedges to serve.

NUTRITIONAL ANALYSIS PER SERVING: Calories 342 (Kilojoules 1,436); Protein 3 g; Carbohydrates 56 g; Total Fat 13 g; Saturated Fat 8 g; Cholesterol 32 mg; Sodium 147 mg; Dietary Fiber 4 g

Apricot and Cinnamon Soufflés

PREP TIME: 20 MINUTES, PLUS
30 MINUTES FOR COOLING

COOKING TIME: 30 MINUTES

INGREDIENTS

½ lb (250 g) dried apricots

1½ cups (12 fl oz/375 ml) water

3 tablespoons amaretto liqueur

1 cinnamon stick

granulated sugar for coating soufflé dishes, plus 3 tablespoons granulated sugar

4 egg whites

pinch of salt

1 tablespoon sliced (flaked) almonds

confectioners' (icing) sugar

ground cinnamon

PREP TIP: To make it easier to assemble, bake, and serve these soufflés, cook and purée the apricots the day ahead. Store the purée at room temperature.

These elegant mini soufflés, made with just a few choice ingredients, are very low in fat. They are best served warm and puffed from the oven, but if they must stand, they will deflate only a little. Even slightly fallen, however, the taste is fabulous.

SERVES 8

❀ In a small saucepan over medium heat, combine the apricots, water, amaretto, and cinnamon stick. Bring to a boil, cover, reduce the heat to low, and cook until the apricots are very soft and most of the liquid is absorbed, about 15 minutes. Remove from the heat and let cool slightly. Remove the cinnamon stick and discard. Transfer the apricots and liquid to a food processor and process until puréed. Transfer to a bowl and let cool.

❀ Position the bottom oven rack at its lowest position and remove the middle rack. Preheat the oven to 400°F (200°C). Lightly butter eight ¾-cup (6-fl oz/180-ml) soufflé dishes. Sprinkle the inside of each dish lightly with a little granulated sugar; tap out the excess.

❀ In a large bowl, using an electric mixer, beat the egg whites with the salt until soft peaks form. Gradually beat in the 3 tablespoons granulated sugar, 1 tablespoon at a time, beating well after each addition. Beat the whites until stiff peaks form.

❀ Fold a spoonful of the whites into the apricot purée to lighten it. Spoon the remaining apricot mixture over the whites and gently fold in just until the mixture is blended. Spoon into the prepared dishes, smoothing the tops with a spatula. Run your fingertip around the rim of each dish, dipping it about ¼ inch (6 mm) into the mixture. This will form a high hat as the soufflé cooks and rises. Sprinkle each soufflé with a few almond slices.

❀ Bake until puffed and golden, 12–15 minutes. Remove from the oven and, using a fine-mesh sieve, quickly sift confectioners' sugar lightly over the soufflés. Sprinkle with a little ground cinnamon. Serve immediately.

NUTRITIONAL ANALYSIS PER SOUFFLÉ: Calories 148 (Kilojoules 622); Protein 3 g; Carbohydrates 30 g; Total Fat 2 g; Saturated Fat 1 g; Cholesterol 3 g; Sodium 48 mg; Dietary Fiber 2 g

GLOSSARY

APPLES, GOLDEN DELICIOUS

With its golden skin, crisp flesh, and sweet-tart flavor, this widely available variety is an excellent all-purpose apple. Pippin, Granny Smith, or Fuji apples are possible substitutes.

BELGIAN ENDIVE

At their peak of season in early winter, these spear-shaped leaves, which are white to pale yellow-green—or sometimes red—at their edges, come tightly packed in cylindrical heads 4–6 inches (10–15 cm) long. They have a crisp texture and a refreshing, slightly bitter flavor that make them excellent additions to holiday salads. The curved leaves are also ideal for stuffing and serving as finger foods. Also known as chicory or witloof.

CAVIARS

Savored for their subtle, briny taste, delicate texture, and shimmering color, salt-preserved fish eggs, or roe, add an extra-special touch to holiday celebrations. The term *caviar* applies strictly to the preserved roe of the sturgeon, a rare and costly product ranging in color from black to gray and at its best in the three premium varieties known as beluga, sevruga, and osetra. Other, less expensive roes are also eaten, and the same term is sometimes loosely extended to them. To duplicate the look of black sturgeon caviars, some cooks turn to inexpensive lumpfish roe, which can be colored black with vegetable dyes. Also popular is salmon roe, large, glossy orange-pink eggs with the distinctive taste of that fish. You can find good selections of caviars and other roes in select specialty-food stores and delicatessens.

CHEESES

Richly satisfying pleasures at any time of year, cheeses add an extra touch of luxury to holiday meals. Those featured in this book include:

CREAM CHEESE

This thick, creamy cheese is appreciated for its rich, mild, slightly tangy flavor and smooth texture. Ideally, use cream cheese that has not been stabilized with an emulsifier.

FONTINA

Made from cow's milk, this popular Italian cheese has a firm, creamy texture and delicate, slightly nutty taste. The best version is produced in Val d'Aosta, a valley in the Italian Alps near Switzerland. The finest is made between May and September and is always labeled with the valley's name.

GOAT CHEESE

Although many different kinds of cheese are made from goat's milk, the most commonly available are fresh and creamy and have a distinctively sharp, tangy flavor. They are sold shaped into small rounds or logs, which are sometimes coated with pepper, ash, or mixtures of herbs. Also known by the French term *chèvre*.

GORGONZOLA

This Italian blue-veined cheese, originating in the town of Gorgonzola near Milan, is prized for its creamy texture and strong, sharp, almost spicy flavor. Milder varieties, which are factory made, are labeled "dolcelatte," literally "sweet milk."

GRUYÈRE

A specific type of Swiss cheese, Gruyère has a relatively strong flavor, firm, smooth texture, small holes, and a reddish brown rind. It makes an excellent cooking cheese.

MOZZARELLA

This rindless Italian white cheese has a mild taste and soft but dense texture. Mozzarella made in the traditional way from water buffalo's milk may be found fresh, immersed in water, in well-stocked food stores and Italian delicatessens. More widely available is packaged cow's milk mozzarella, which tends to be drier and less flavorful. If only cow's milk mozzarella is available, look for balls sold in water rather than dry-packed in plastic.

PARMESAN

Aged for at least 2 years until it has a firm texture, a thick crust, and a sharp, salty flavor, this cheese from the area around Parma is commonly used as a seasoning, grated over pasta. Buy it in block form, to grate fresh as needed. The finest variety is designated Parmigiano-Reggiano®.

PECORINO

The term *pecorino* applies throughout Italy to any cheese made from sheep's milk, but it usually refers to the aged variety known as pecorino romano, produced in the region around Rome. It is piquant in flavor and often used as a grating cheese.

RICOTTA

This light-textured, white, very mild cheese, used in savory and sweet recipes, is produced from whey left over from making other cheeses. Sheep's milk is the traditional base, although cow's milk ricotta is more common.

CRANBERRIES

Perhaps the definitive American fruit of the holiday season, these round, deep red, tart berries grow primarily in wet, sandy coastal lands—or bogs—in the Northeast and Midwest. Available fresh during late autumn, cranberries can be found frozen year-round.

DRIED FRUITS

Bringing with them memories of earlier times, when cooks relied on home-preserved foods in winter, many varieties of dried fruit have become traditional additions to cold-weather holiday dishes, adding their concentrated flavor and chewy texture to sweet and savory recipes alike. Among the most commonly available types are dried apples, apricots, Mission and Calimyrna figs, prunes, and raisins, which may be found in most food stores. You may have to search a bit more to find dried currants or cherries, although they are available with increasing frequency in well-stocked and specialty-food stores. Try to select more recently dried and packaged fruits, which will have a softer texture than older dried fruits.

GARLIC

Prized for its pungent and highly aromatic taste, garlic is an indispensable ingredient in many savory dishes. For the best flavor, buy whole heads of dried garlic, separating individual cloves from the head as you need them. Do not buy more than you will use in 1 to 2 weeks.

To peel a garlic clove, place it on a work surface and press down firmly on it with the side of a knife blade, the bottom of a saucepan,

or some other heavy object. The papery skin will loosen and slip off easily. This action also "bruises" a whole garlic clove, keeping it intact while helping to release its flavorful oils before it is added to a recipe.

GINGER

Although it resembles a root, this sweet-hot seasoning is actually the underground stem, or rhizome, of the tropical ginger plant. It is sold fresh and in a dried ground form. Ginger pieces are also sold crystallized—that is, candied with sugar—in specialty-food shops and well-stocked food stores.

HERBS

Herbs add bright color and lively flavor to holiday dishes. To store fresh herbs, refrigerate them, either with their stem ends in a glass of water or wrapped in damp paper towels inside a plastic bag. Buy dried herbs in quantities no greater than you would use in a few months, storing them airtight and away from light and heat.

BASIL

Spicy-sweet, tender-leaved basil, an indispensable seasoning of the Mediterranean kitchen, goes especially well in dishes that feature tomatoes. It also complements a wide variety of sauces and poultry dishes.

BAY LEAF

The dried whole leaves of the bay laurel tree impart a pungent, spicy flavor to long-simmered dishes such as soups and stews.

Seek out Turkish bay leaves, which have a milder, sweeter flavor than bay grown in California.

CHIVE

This mild, sweet, deep green herb has a flavor reminiscent of the onion, to which it is related. It delivers color and a pleasingly subtle pungency both as a seasoning and a garnish. For the best flavor, add chives near the end of cooking or to the finished dish, as heat diminishes their flavor.

DILL

Fine, feathery fresh dill leaves have a delicately sweet, aromatic flavor that complements egg and seafood dishes and cooked vegetables such as carrots and potatoes.

PARSLEY, FLAT-LEAF

Also known as Italian parsley, this variety of the widely popular fresh herb, native to southern Europe, has a more pronounced flavor than the curly variety, which makes it preferable as a seasoning. Choose only those bunches with bright green leaves and no evidence of wilting. Because parsley marries well with most savory foods, it is a holiday pantry staple.

ROSEMARY

The needle-shaped leaves of this Mediterranean herb have a strong, aromatic character. Used either fresh or dried, it's ideal for meats, poultry, seafood, and vegetables.

SAGE

The oval, gray-green leaves of this popular Mediterranean herb have a distinctively sweet flavor and fragrance reminiscent of anise with a lightly musty edge. Use it, fresh or dried, to complement poultry, stuffings, pork, and bean dishes.

TARRAGON

Used both fresh and dried, this herb has a distinctively sweet flavor. A classic seasoning for roast chicken and other poultry, it also goes well with eggs and seafood.

THYME

A brightly flavored ancient herb of the eastern Mediterranean, thyme may be used fresh or dried to flavor vegetables and poultry, seafood, and egg dishes. It is also a classic addition to a bouquet garni, a bunch of herbs bound together and used as a flavoring for soups and stews.

NUTS

The mellow flavor and crunchy texture of nuts enhance many holiday dishes. For the best selection, look in specialty-food shops, health-food stores, or the baking section of food markets. Some popular holiday options include mellow, sweet **almonds**, commonly sold sliced (flaked) or skinless (blanched) and cut into slivers; kidney-shaped **cashews**, enjoyed for their buttery, slightly sweet taste; small, spherical **hazelnuts** *(above right)*, also known as filberts, prized for their rich, slightly sweet flavor with a pleasant hint of bitterness; brown-skinned, crinkly surfaced, rich pecans; and rich, crisp **walnuts**, of which the English variety is best-known and most widely available. The American black walnut, usually sold as shelled pieces, has a stronger flavor, however, and is preferred in holiday desserts and candies.

OILS

Rich in both taste and texture, oils add to the festivity of many a holiday meal. **Olive oil**, in particular, has links tracing back to biblical times and plays a significant part in both Jewish and Christian traditions. **Extra-virgin olive oil** is the highest grade, extracted on the first-pressing of ripe olives without use of heat or chemicals. It has a distinctively fruity flavor and color that will vary depending upon the particular olives pressed. It is used primarily to contribute character to dressings or marinades or as a condiment. Products

MUSHROOMS

Earthy in flavor, mushrooms add rich, robust character to many holiday dishes. To clean fresh mushrooms of any soil adhering to their surfaces, gently brush them with a small, soft-bristled brush or a lightly dampened paper towel.

CHANTERELLES

Wild mushrooms now also cultivated commercially, these firm-fleshed, pale yellow specimens are shaped like a furled trumpet. They are distinguished by their mild flavor.

CREMINI

These mushrooms resemble common cultivated mushrooms in their shape and size, but they are richer in flavor and have a medium brown skin and deep ivory flesh.

MORELS

Noted for their cylindrical, dark brown caps and rich earthy flavor, these wild mushrooms can be found fresh in spring- and summertime, or are available dried year-round.

PORCINI

Prized for their meaty texture and rich flavor, porcini are found fresh in summer and autumn. Dried porcini are sold in Italian delicatessens and specialty-food stores. Also known as *cèpes.*

PORTOBELLOS

The flat, circular brown caps of these mushrooms *(above right)*, the fully matured form of cremini, grow up to 4 inches (10 cm) or more in diameter. They are enjoyed for their rich taste and texture when cooked.

SHIITAKE

These are prized for their rich flavor and chewy texture, whether fresh or dried and reconstituted in warm water. Their flat circular caps have a distinctive velvety dark brown color.

WHITE

These are mild-tasting, with white caps and short stems. Immature white mushrooms with caps that have not yet opened are sometimes called button mushrooms.

labeled "pure olive oil" have undergone further filtering to eliminate much of their aroma and flavor, and are better suited to general cooking purposes. Other vegetable and seed oils such as **canola, safflower,** and **corn oil,** generally referred to in recipes as "**vegetable oil,**" have bland flavors that impart no distinctive character of their own and may be heated without burning to the high temperatures necessary for frying.

SHALLOTS

These brown-skinned, purple-tinged cousins of onions and garlic, midway in size and shape between the two, are also thought by some to have a flavor resembling a cross between their well-known kin.

VINEGARS

Tangy vinegars made from wine, apple cider, and other alcoholic liquids add a lively splash of flavor to dressings, marinades, and sauces. All vinegars, apart from characterless distilled white vinegar, will have distinctive flavors based on the products from which they have been made. The best-quality **wine vinegars** derive from good-quality wine, with red wine vinegars having a more robust flavor than those produced from white wine. **Champagne vinegar** has a pale color and a delicate flavor, making it an elegant substitute in recipes that call for white wine vinegar. **Balsamic vinegar** is made from reduced grape juice and aged for many years in casks made from a variety of woods. **Sherry vinegar** has a rich flavor and color reminiscent of the fortified, cask-aged wine that gives it its name. **Cider vinegar** has a rich appley tang, while **rice wine vinegar** is clean and light in taste. **Flavored vinegars** are made by adding herbs such as tarragon and fruits or fruit syrups to wine vinegars.

ZEST

The outermost, brightly colored layer of a citrus fruit's rind, rich in essential oils that literally add zest to savory and sweet dishes. Zest may be removed in several ways: in

SPICES

Spices add a lively, often exotic character to holiday dishes. Buy all spices in small quantities from a store that has a rapid turnover of inventory, as flavors tend to diminish rapidly. Store in airtight containers away from heat and light. For the best flavor, when possible buy spices as whole seeds and use an electric spice mill or a mortar and pestle to grind them as needed.

ALLSPICE

This sweet Caribbean spice, sold ground or as whole dried berries, gets its name because its flavor resembles a blend of cinnamon, cloves, and nutmeg.

CAYENNE PEPPER

Prized for its hot taste and bright red color, this fine powder is ground from the dried cayenne chile.

CINNAMON

One of the most popular spices for holiday baked goods and other desserts, cinnamon is the aromatic bark of a type of evergreen tree. It may be bought either ground or as whole dried and curled strips of bark, known as cinnamon sticks.

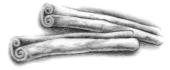

CLOVES

Native to Southeast Asia, these dried flower buds of an evergreen tree have a rich, highly aromatic flavor and may be used whole or ground.

particles with a fine grater; in strips with a vegetable peeler or a "stripper"; or in fine shreds with the small, sharp-edged holes of a "zester." In any case, take care not to remove any of the bitter white pith beneath the zest.

CUMIN SEEDS

Small, crescent-shaped cumin seeds, favored in Middle Eastern, Indian, and Mexican kitchens, add a strong, dusky aroma to savory dishes.

CURRY POWDER, MADRAS

The term *curry powder* refers to complex Indian spice blends usually including coriander, cumin, chile, fenugreek, and turmeric; cardamom, cinnamon, cloves, allspice, fennel seeds, and ginger are also common components. Products labeled "Madras" curry powder refer to fairly hot blends popular in India's southeastern region of that name, with a greater emphasis placed on such sweet, hot, and pungent spices as fenugreek, coriander, cumin, turmeric, mace, ginger, and chile.

JUNIPER BERRIES

These small, dried berries of the juniper tree have a resinous scent reminiscent of gin, which they flavor. They are used principally for seasoning meats and sauces.

NUTMEG

The hard pit of the fruit of the nutmeg tree, this popular sweet spice adds a subtle dimension of flavor to both sweet and savory holiday dishes. Nutmeg may be bought already ground, but the freshest, fullest flavor comes from whole nutmeg that you grate yourself. Whole nutmegs may be stored inside special nutmeg graters, which include hinged flaps that conceal a storage compartment.

INDEX

ACKNOWLEDGMENTS

The publishers would like to thank the following people and associations for their generous assistance and support in
producing this book: Sharylin Hovind, Ken DellaPenta, and Hill Nutrition Associates.

The following kindly lent props for photography: Fillamento, Williams-Sonoma, and Pottery Barn, San Francisco, CA. The photographer would like to
thank Jeff Tucker, Kevin Hossler, and John and Dawn Owen for generously sharing their homes with us for our location settings. We would also like to
thank Chromeworks and Procamera, San Francisco, CA, and FUJI Film, for their generous support of this project. Special acknowledgment goes to
Daniel Yearwood for the beautiful backgrounds and surface treatments.

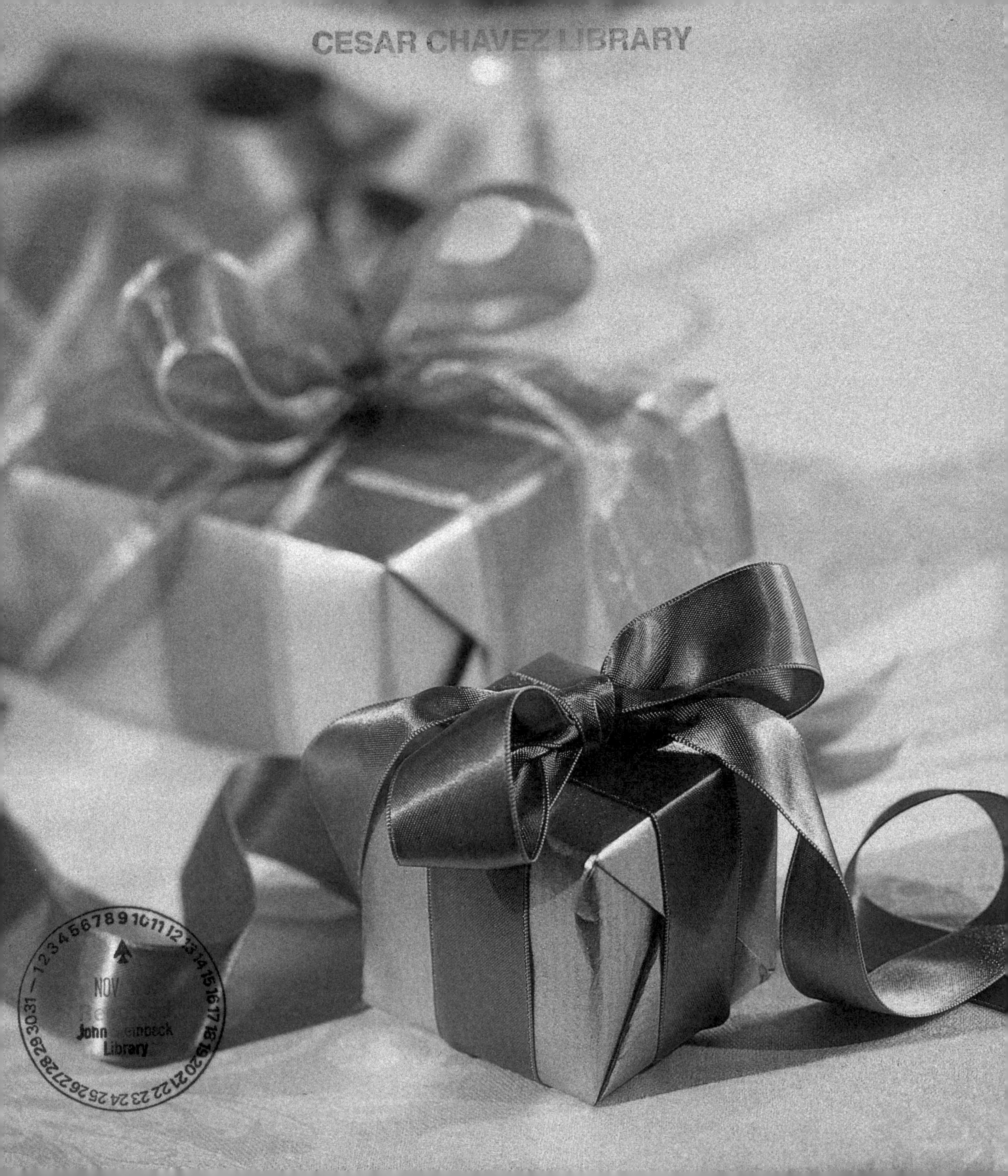